OFFICIAL

PAST PAPERS WITH ANSWERS

HIGHER

FRENCH
2008-2012

First exam published in 2008.
Published by Bright Red Publishing Ltd, 6 Stafford Street, Edinburgh EH3 7AU
tel: 0131 220 5804 fax: 0131 220 6710 info@brightredpublishing.co.uk www.brightredpublishing.co.uk

ISBN 978-1-84948-287-5

A CIP Catalogue record for this book is available from the British Library.

Bright Red Publishing is grateful to the copyright holders, as credited on the final page of the Question Section, for permission to use their material. Every effort has been made to trace the copyright holders and to obtain their permission for the use of copyright material. Bright Red Publishing will be happy to receive information allowing us to rectify any error or omission in future editions.

HIGHER

2008

[BLANK PAGE]

X059/301

NATIONAL
QUALIFICATIONS
2008

WEDNESDAY, 21 MAY
9.00 AM – 10.40 AM

FRENCH
HIGHER
Reading and
Directed Writing

45 marks are allocated to this paper. The value attached to each question is shown after each question.

You should spend approximately one hour on Section I and 40 minutes on Section II.

You may use a French dictionary.

SECTION I—READING

Read this article carefully and answer **in English** the questions which follow it.

In this passage, Camille describes how her blog (her on-line diary) changed her life.

Comment mon blog a changé ma vie

C'est Andy Warhol qui le disait: "À l'avenir, chacun aura son quart d'heure de célébrité". Moi, je suis célèbre depuis plus de quatre mois. Et qu'ai-je 5 fait pour mériter cette renommée? J'ai tout simplement ouvert mon blog sur internet.

C'est par pure jalousie que j'ai commencé mon blog. Je venais de voir 10 celui de mon amie Anuja, intitulé «Studious in the City». Avec une photo très élégante à la page d'accueil, où elle apparaît bien maquillée et avec son large sourire, Anuja a rejoint la cohorte 15 de «blogueurs» qui apparaissent sur le Net depuis 1999. Et pourquoi pas moi?

Me and the City

J'ai donc ouvert mon propre blog, 20 «La Gazette new-yorkaise», où je raconte les événements de ma vie d'étudiante de journalisme à l'université de New York. Tous les trois jours, j'écris, par exemple, une 25 critique de l'exposition de Van Gogh au Metropolitan Museum; je mets en doute la candidature de la ville de New York pour les Jeux Olympiques de 2012; ou je décris ma rencontre avec 30 une patrouille de la police dans les rues de Harlem. J'illustre chaque article de photos réalisées avec mon appareil photo numérique[1].

Les Français adorent tout ce qui 35 touche à New York, et j'apporte à mes lecteurs, via mon blog, un peu de l'ambiance new-yorkaise. Ces lecteurs sont en moyenne 200 par jour, et certains sont devenus des habitués et apprécient mes efforts. Bruno, de 40 Saint-Étienne, m'a écrit, «Je surfe de blog en blog. Le tien est sensass. Les descriptions de tes soirées nous offrent une petite tranche de la vie new-yorkaise». Ces commentaires flattent 45 mon ego: les premiers jours, j'avais vraiment l'impression d'être une superstar du Net.

Attention au blog!

Hélas, être un personnage «public» 50 n'est pas toujours agréable. J'ai découvert les dangers de donner de nombreux détails sur ma vie privée à n'importe quel inconnu qui tape au hasard des mots dans leur moteur de 55 recherche. Comme, par exemple, une certaine Élodie qui m'a demandé des conseils pour étudier dans une université américaine. Honorée, j'ai rédigé une réponse complète, où je lui 60 ai tout expliqué. Mais cela ne lui a pas suffi. En moins de quarante-huit heures, Élodie m'avait envoyé cinq autres e-mails. Quand j'ai cessé tout contact, son ton est devenu de moins 65 en moins cordial et j'ai enfin souffert un torrent d'insultes et de menaces.

Heureusement, une fois ces frayeurs passées, une bonne surprise m'attendait. Un journaliste anglais du 70 «Daily Telegraph» m'a contactée après avoir lu un commentaire sur mon blog à propos du film «Les Choristes». Le journaliste devait interviewer Jean-Baptiste Maunier, la star du film, 75 et souhaitait me parler. Ce que j'ai fait. Une offre d'emploi a suivi. Vraiment, mon blog a changé ma vie.

Je suis devenue «blog-addict»!

80 Désormais, le moment où je me réveille, je consulte compulsivement les statistiques de visiteurs à mon blog. Je déteste les jours où personne ne fait de commentaires, et je suis enchantée dès

85 qu'un nouveau lecteur se manifeste. Je ne cesse pas d'améliorer mon blog.

Mais malheureusement, cette aventure virtuelle va bientôt prendre fin, avec mon retour imminent en France. Dans mon arrogance, je pense que mes 90 lecteurs seront inconsolables. Mais j'ai déjà la solution: je vais commencer mon nouveau blog à Paris. J'ai déjà trouvé le nom: «La Gazette parisienne».

[1] un appareil photo numérique = a digital camera

QUESTIONS

Marks

1. A large number of blogs (on-line diaries) have sprung up since 1999. (lines 1–17)

   (a) What prompted Camille to start her blog? — **1 point**

   (b) How had Anuja tried to make her blog immediately attractive? — **2 points**

2. On her blog, Camille writes about her life in New York. (lines 18–48)

   (a) Give details of the kinds of thing that Camille puts on her blog. — **3 points**

   (b) Why, in her opinion, do her readers find her site interesting? — **1 point**

   (c) Why did Bruno think her site was great? — **1 point**

   (d) How does Camille react to comments such as his? — **1 point**

3. There are also dangers in having your own blog. (lines 49–67)

   (a) What did Camille realise is a dangerous thing to do? — **1 point**

   (b) What happened after Camille gave Élodie the information that she asked for? — **3 points**

4. Camille's blog has had a major impact upon her life. (lines 68–94)

   (a) Why did a journalist from the Daily Telegraph contact her? — **2 points**

   (b) What eventual benefit did this bring Camille? — **1 point**

   (c) What shows how far Camille has become addicted to her blog? — **3 points**

   (d) Why does she describe herself as arrogant? — **1 point**

   (20 points)

   = 20 marks

5. Translate into English:

   "C'est Andy Warhol . . . ouvert mon blog sur internet." (lines 1–7) — **10**

   (30)

[Turn over for SECTION II on *Page four*

SECTION II—DIRECTED WRITING

Marks

Last summer you and a group of fellow-students went on a study trip to your twin town, to find out more about it.

On your return from the visit, you have been asked to write an account of your experiences **in French** for inclusion in the foreign language section of your school/college magazine.

You must include the following information and **you should try to add** other relevant details:

* where your twin town is **and** whether you had visited it before
* where you stayed **and** what you thought of the accommodation
* what you did during your stay to find out more about the town
* what you liked **or** disliked about the town
* what you thought of the people that you met during your stay
* how other students in your school/college will benefit from your visit.

Your account should be 150–180 words in length.

Marks will be deducted for any area of information that is omitted.   (15)

[END OF QUESTION PAPER]

X059/303

NATIONAL
QUALIFICATIONS
2008

WEDNESDAY, 21 MAY
11.00 AM – 12.00 NOON

FRENCH
HIGHER
Listening Transcript

This paper must not be seen by any candidate.

The material overleaf is provided for use in an emergency only (eg the recording or equipment proving faulty) or where permission has been given in advance by SQA for the material to be read to candidates with additional support needs. The material must be read exactly as printed.

Instructions to reader(s):

Candidates have two minutes to study the questions before the transcript is read.

The dialogue below should be read in approximately 4 minutes. On completion of the first reading, pause for two minutes, then read the dialogue a second time.

Where special arrangements have been agreed in advance to allow the reading of the material, those sections marked **(f)** should be read by a female speaker and those marked **(m)** by a male.

Francine is talking about the part-time jobs that she has had.

(m)   **Francine, aviez-vous un job à temps partiel quand vous étiez étudiante?**

(f)   Oui, en effet j'avais deux jobs. Deux fois par semaine je travaillais le soir comme serveuse dans un restaurant et le mercredi soir je gardais des petits enfants. Travailler le soir est certes difficile, mais c'est mieux payé que de travailler pendant la journée.

(m)   **Pourquoi aviez-vous décidé de trouver un job?**

(f)   C'était pour financer mes journées shopping, car j'adore faire les magasins. Aussi, je voulais découvrir le monde du travail.

(m)   **Aviez-vous une préférence entre les deux jobs?**

(f)   Je préférais mon travail avec les enfants le mercredi car je pouvais jouer avec eux et, quand ils dormaient, je pouvais faire mes devoirs et étudier. D'autre part, mon job au restaurant était plutôt fatigant. Pour être serveuse, il faut sourire tout le temps.

(m)   **Comment étaient les clients au restaurant?**

(f)   En général, ils étaient gentils avec moi. Ils étaient de bonne humeur parce qu'ils venaient au restaurant pour s'amuser en famille ou avec leurs amis. Et d'habitude ils me laissaient de bons pourboires.

(m)   **Et les collègues dans le restaurant? Ils étaient sympas?**

(f)   Je m'entendais plutôt bien avec eux. La plupart d'entre eux étaient du même âge que moi, et ils travaillaient pour les mêmes raisons. Je suis restée en contact avec plusieurs d'entre eux, et quelques-uns sont même devenus de très bons amis.

(m)   **Y avait-il des aspects de ces jobs que vous avez trouvés difficiles?**

(f)   Il était difficile de me motiver après une longue journée d'études. Et garder des enfants apporte beaucoup de responsabilité et demande énormément d'attention.

(m)   **Et, qu'est-ce que vos parents pensaient de votre décision de trouver un job?**

(f)   Mes parents n'étaient pas très contents. Pour eux, les études passent avant tout et ils pensaient que mes études allaient en souffrir. Mais ils avaient tort, car j'ai fait des études supplémentaires le week-end, et j'ai cessé de travailler dans le restaurant quand mes examens s'approchaient.

(m)   **Tout bien considéré, vous avez profité des jobs?**

(f)   Oui, bien sûr. Les jobs m'ont apporté du bonheur, ce qui est bien plus important que de gagner de l'argent. Les enfants étaient adorables et je les revois toujours. Ils ont grandi, mais ils se rappellent toujours de moi. Pour moi, c'est ça l'important.

[END OF TRANSCRIPT]

[BLANK PAGE]

FOR OFFICIAL USE

Examiner's Marks	
A	
B	

Total Mark

X059/302

NATIONAL
QUALIFICATIONS
2008

WEDNESDAY, 21 MAY
11.00 AM – 12.00 NOON

FRENCH
HIGHER
Listening/Writing

Fill in these boxes and read what is printed below.

Full name of centre

Town

Forename(s)

Surname

Date of birth

Day   Month   Year   Scottish candidate number   Number of seat

Do not open this paper until told to do so.

Answer Section A **in English** and Section B **in French**.

Section A

Listen carefully to the recording with a view to answering, **in English**, the questions printed in this answer book. Write your answers **clearly and legibly** in the spaces provided after each question.

You will have 2 minutes to study the questions before hearing the dialogue for the first time.

The dialogue will be played **twice**, with an interval of 2 minutes between the two playings.

You may make notes at any time but only in this answer book. **Draw your pen through any notes before you hand in the book.**

Move on to Section B when you have completed Section A: you will **not** be told when to do this.

Section B

Do not write your response in this book: **use the 4 page lined answer sheet**.

You will be told to insert the answer sheet inside this book before handing in your work.

You may consult a French dictionary at any time during **both** sections.

Before leaving the examination room you must give this book to the invigilator. If you do not, you may lose all the marks for this paper.

Section A

Marks

Francine is talking about the part-time jobs that she has had.

1. (*a*) Francine had two evening jobs. What were they and how often did she do them?

2 points

(*b*) What does Francine say is the advantage of working in the evening?

1 point

2. Why had Francine decided to get a job?

2 points

3. She liked one job better than the other.

(*a*) Why did she prefer that job?

2 points

(*b*) What did she not like about the other job?

2 points

4. (*a*) Why were her customers in a good mood?

1 point

Marks

4.   **(continued)**

   (b) How did she benefit from this?   **1 point**

5.   Why did Francine and her fellow workers get on well together?   **2 points**

6.   What aspects of her job did Francine find difficult?   **2 points**

7.   (a) What concern did her parents have about Francine's jobs?   **1 point**

   (b) What did Francine do to meet this concern?   **2 points**

8.   According to Francine, how has she benefited from her jobs?   **2 points**

(20 points)
= 20 marks

[Turn over for Section B on *Page four*

Marks

Section B

Les jobs de Francine lui ont apporté de l'argent. Est-ce que vous avez assez d'argent pour vos besoins? A votre avis, quels sont les avantages et les inconvénients d'avoir un emploi à temps partiel?

Ecrivez 120–150 mots en français pour exprimer vos idées.

10

(30)

USE THE 4 PAGE LINED ANSWER SHEET FOR YOUR ANSWER TO SECTION B

[END OF QUESTION PAPER]

HIGHER

2009

[BLANK PAGE]

X059/301

NATIONAL
QUALIFICATIONS
2009

FRIDAY, 22 MAY
9.00 AM – 10.40 AM

FRENCH
HIGHER
Reading and
Directed Writing

45 marks are allocated to this paper. The value attached to each question is shown after each question.

You should spend approximately one hour on Section I and 40 minutes on Section II.

You may use a French dictionary.

SECTION I—READING

Read the whole article carefully and then answer **in English** the questions which follow it.

This passage tells us about homeless people who live in the woods surrounding Paris.

Ils vivent dans les bois, été comme hiver!

Tout autour de Paris, environ 500 personnes vivent dans les bois car ils n'ont pas de domicile fixe. Dans l'ouest de la capitale, près du joli petit
5 village de Chaville, vous verrez deux mondes bien différents: d'un côté de la route, les résidences chics des habitants de banlieue; de l'autre, un campement où survivent avec difficulté les gens des
10 bois.

C'est là que Fernando et David se sont installés. «En fait, nous sommes une bonne dizaine à habiter dans ce coin du bois en groupes de deux ou
15 trois», dit David. «Il n'y a jamais de disputes entre nous: éloignés les uns des autres, chaque groupe a son propre territoire.» Ces deux hommes ont construit une petite cabane, faite de ce
20 que les habitants du village ont jeté. «Elle est assez solide pour résister à un vent de 80 km/h», dit Fernando avec fierté. A l'intérieur, les lits déjà faits et les couvertures bien rangées dans un
25 coin reflètent l'amour-propre[1] des deux hommes. Au milieu de la cabane, une belle table élégante, mais cassée, qu'ils ont récupérée aux dépôts de déchets de Chaville.

30 A proximité, on aperçoit la niche de leurs chiens, deux beaux animaux qui montent la garde. Un peu plus loin ils ont leur petit jardin potager: pas facile de faire pousser des légumes en pleine
35 forêt, mais ils y arrivent. Nettoyé de ses branches et feuilles, le terrain autour de leur cabane est devenu leur espace repos.

Un problème pas facile à résoudre
40

Pourtant, la municipalité n'a pas abandonné ces hommes. «On fait ce qu'on peut pour les aider, mais ce n'est pas facile», explique une représentante du Conseil Régional d'Ile-de-France.
45 «Ils mènent une vie très isolée, et souvent ils n'acceptent pas volontiers l'assistance des pouvoirs publics. A Chaville, nous avons ouvert un centre où ils peuvent venir chaque semaine
50 prendre un bon petit déjeuner et utiliser la machine à laver. Quand ils viennent au centre à Noël, on leur offre un colis. Mais nous n'avons pas de solution permanente à leur offrir. Il y a
55 de moins en moins de logements à prix modéré disponibles: non seulement on n'en construit plus, mais on démolit ceux qui existent.»

Autre difficulté, c'est qu'ils ne
60 trouvent pas facilement du travail. Les petites entreprises se méfient d'eux, précisément parce qu'ils n'ont pas de domicile fixe. Ils sont donc obligés d'accepter un jour par-ci, un autre jour
65 par-là, soit dans les chantiers, soit comme travailleurs saisonniers.

«Regardez comme tout est propre ici ! »

«Des fois, quand on va en ville, les
70 gens nous menacent», reprend David. «Ils disent que nous sommes sales. Pour éviter cela, il faut que nous soyons toujours très propres. Il y a une source d'eau pas loin d'ici où nous
75 lavons régulièrement notre linge, à la

main. Ça va en été, mais en hiver, qu'est-ce qu'on a froid! La galère[2], c'est pour s'éclairer et se chauffer. Les 80 bougies, c'est pas pratique, car on court le risque de mettre feu à la cabane. L'hiver, pour se réchauffer, on fait un feu de bois à côté de la cabane; mais, évidemment, ça fait des problèmes 85 quand il se met à pleuvoir.»

Parfois le soir, Fernando et David s'installent auprès de leur petite table devant leur cabane et à l'écart des chemins empruntés par les familles en balade. Ils passent une heure à 90 discuter tranquillement. Certes, leur vie est difficile, mais malgré tout elle permet des moments d'amitié. Quand le temps s'y prête . . . !

[1] l'amour-propre = the self-respect
[2] la galère = the hardest part/the worst thing

Marks

QUESTIONS

1. Hundreds of homeless people live in the woods around Paris. (lines 1–38)

   (a) What two "worlds" does the author describe? **2 points**

   (b) Why are there never any arguments among the groups of men who live in the woods? **1 point**

   (c) Why is Fernando proud of his shack? **1 point**

   (d) How does the shack's interior reflect Fernando and David's self-respect? **1 point**

   (e) The two men recycle some of society's waste. Give **two** examples of this from lines 1–38. **2 points**

2. The authorities are finding it difficult to meet the needs of these homeless people. (lines 39–67)

   (a) What makes it hard for the Regional Council to help men like Fernando and David? **2 points**

   (b) What does the centre in Chaville do throughout the year to improve the men's lives? **2 points**

   (c) Why is there a lack of low-cost housing available for people in this situation? **2 points**

   (d) Why can it be difficult for such men to find work? **1 point**

   (e) What types of work might they have to accept? **2 points**

3. Fernando and David have managed to solve most practical problems. (lines 68–85) What problems do they still face with:

   (a) washing their clothes? **1 point**

   (b) lighting? **1 point**

   (c) heating? **1 point**

4. Most local families are unaware of the men's existence. (lines 86–94)

   What is the author's final comment on the men's lifestyle? **1 point**
   (20 points)
   = 20 marks

5. Translate into English:

   A proximité . . . mais ils y arrivent. (lines 30–35) **10**

   [Turn over for SECTION II on *Page four* **(30)**

SECTION II—DIRECTED WRITING

Marks

Last year, you had a holiday job in France.

On your return from the visit, you have been asked to write an account of your experiences **in French** for inclusion in the foreign language section of your school/college magazine.

You must include the following information and **you should try to add** other relevant details:

- why you applied for the job, **and** what part of France it was in
- what your accommodation was like **and** how you travelled to work
- what you did during the working day
- how you got on with the other people you worked with
- what you liked or did not like about the job
- what you plan to do with the money that you earned.

Your account should be 150–180 words in length.

Marks will be deducted for any area of information that is omitted.   (15)

[END OF QUESTION PAPER]

X059/303

NATIONAL QUALIFICATIONS 2009	FRIDAY, 22 MAY 11.00 AM – 12.00 NOON	**FRENCH HIGHER** Listening Transcript

This paper must not be seen by any candidate.

The material overleaf is provided for use in an emergency only (eg the recording or equipment proving faulty) or where permission has been given in advance by SQA for the material to be read to candidates with additional support needs. The material must be read exactly as printed.

Instructions to reader(s):

The dialogue below should be read in approximately 4 minutes. On completion of the first reading, pause for two minutes, then read the dialogue a second time.

Where special arrangements have been agreed in advance to allow the reading of the material, those sections marked **(f)** should be read by a female speaker and those marked **(m)** by a male.

Candidates have two minutes to study the questions before the transcript is read.

Cécile is explaining why she has come back to Scotland as a French Assistant for a second year.

(m) Cécile, vous avez choisi de retourner en Ecosse passer une deuxième année comme assistante française. Pourquoi?

(f) J'ai choisi de retourner en Ecosse car j'ai passé une année merveilleuse l'année dernière. C'était dans un collège à la campagne. Cette année j'ai voulu habiter en ville pour avoir une expérience différente.

(m) Vous connaissez les Ecossais un peu mieux maintenant?

(f) Oui. J'ai fait la connaissance de gens fabuleux et c'est quand on se fait des amis qu'on commence vraiment à connaître leur culture. En plus, vivre en Ecosse m'a permis de décider plus précisément de ce que je vais faire comme carrière.

(m) Ça vous intéresserait de travailler comme professeur à l'avenir?

(f) Oui, je voudrais être professeur dans un collège en France. Après mes expériences dans la salle de classe comme assistante de langues, je comprends mieux ce que c'est le métier d'enseignant: c'est vraiment un travail plus difficile qu'on ne le croit, et qui demande beaucoup de patience et de compréhension.

(m) Vous avez aimé travailler avec les jeunes gens?

(f) Oui. Ce qui m'attire le plus c'est le contact avec les élèves. Je me passionne pour les langues. Mon but principal serait de partager cette passion avec les élèves. Il faut dire que j'ai appris des leçons très pratiques, par exemple comment organiser des classes, et comment éviter les problèmes de discipline.

(m) Pourquoi avez-vous choisi l'Ecosse?

(f) Comme j'ai déjà dit, j'adore l'anglais. C'est mon rêve depuis toute petite fille d'aller vivre dans un pays où l'on parle anglais. Deuxièmement, j'ai toujours voulu voir les paysages écossais, qui sont vraiment magnifiques. Les montagnes écossaises sont les plus spectaculaires du monde. En plus, je m'intéresse beaucoup à l'histoire de l'Ecosse.

(m) **Qu'est-ce que vous n'aimez pas de l'Ecosse ou même des Ecossais?**

(f) Ce que je n'aime pas en Ecosse, c'est le temps! Il pleut trop, et je suis toujours enrhumée! Je me sens parfois déprimée à cause du froid et de la pluie. En plus, je sais que la nourriture écossaise est mauvaise pour la santé mais je l'aime quand même. Enfin, ce que je n'aime pas chez les Ecossais, c'est qu'ils jettent des papiers par terre même s'il y a une poubelle tout près.

(m) **Est-ce que vos parents et vos amis en France vous manquent?**

(f) Ils me manquent énormément! Mes parents me téléphonent chaque semaine et avec mes amis je parle souvent sur MSN. Mais c'est mon chat qui me manque le plus. Quand je suis en France, il est toujours content de me voir quand je rentre le soir.

(m) **Et dites-nous finalement: y a-t-il un petit quelque chose de la France qui vous manque?**

(f) Oui, bien sûr! Les magasins. En France, ils restent ouverts plus tard — jusqu'à 20 heures. C'est bien mieux pour faire du shopping et il faut dire qu'il y a un plus grand choix de vêtements élégants.

[END OF TRANSCRIPT]

[BLANK PAGE]

FOR OFFICIAL USE

Examiner's Marks	
A	
B	

Total
Mark

X059/302

NATIONAL
QUALIFICATIONS
2009

FRIDAY, 22 MAY
11.00 AM – 12.00 NOON

FRENCH
HIGHER
Listening/Writing

Fill in these boxes and read what is printed below.

Full name of centre

Town

Forename(s)

Surname

Date of birth
Day Month Year   Scottish candidate number   Number of seat

Do not open this paper until told to do so.

Answer Section A **in English** and Section B **in French**.

Section A

Listen carefully to the recording with a view to answering, **in English**, the questions printed in this answer book. Write your answers **clearly and legibly** in the spaces provided after each question.

You will have 2 minutes to study the questions before hearing the dialogue for the first time.

The dialogue will be played **twice**, with an interval of 2 minutes between the two playings.

You may make notes at any time but only in this answer book. **Score out any notes before you hand in the book**.

Move on to Section B when you have completed Section A: you will **not** be told when to do this.

Section B

Do not write your response in this book: **use the 4 page lined answer sheet**.

You will be told to insert the answer sheet inside this book before handing in your work.

You may consult a French dictionary at any time during **both** sections.

Before leaving the examination room you must give this book to the invigilator. If you do not, you may lose all the marks for this paper.

Marks

Section A

Cécile is explaining why she has come back to Scotland as a French Assistant for a second year.

1. Why has Cécile decided to come back to Scotland for a second year?   **2 points**

2. (*a*) What really helped her to get to know the culture?   **1 point**

    (*b*) In what other way has living in Scotland helped her?   **1 point**

3. What have her experiences in the classroom taught her about the job of a teacher?   **2 points**

4. (*a*) As a teacher, what would be her main aim for her pupils?   **1 point**

    (*b*) What practical lessons has she herself learned?   **2 points**

Marks

5.   Why was she especially attracted to Scotland?   **3 points**

6.   (a) What effect does the Scottish weather have on her?   **1 point**

     (b) What does she think of Scottish food?   **1 point**

     (c) What does she dislike about the Scottish people?   **1 point**

7.   (a) How does she keep in touch with people in France?   **2 points**

     (b) Why does she miss her cat so much?   **1 point**

8.   What does she say she misses about the shops in France, and why?   **2 points**

                                                                    (20 points)
                                                                    = 20 marks

[Turn over for Section B on *Page four*

Marks

Section B

Cécile a bien aimé son séjour en Ecosse.   A votre avis quels sont les avantages/désavantages de vivre en Ecosse?   Vous pensez aussi qu'il est important de visiter d'autres pays?

Ecrivez 120-150 mots en français pour exprimer vos idées.

10

(30)

USE THE 4 PAGE LINED ANSWER SHEET FOR YOUR ANSWER TO SECTION B

[END OF QUESTION PAPER]

HIGHER

2010

[BLANK PAGE]

X059/301

NATIONAL
QUALIFICATIONS
2010

TUESDAY, 18 MAY
9.00 AM – 10.40 AM

FRENCH
HIGHER
Reading and
Directed Writing

45 marks are allocated to this paper. The value attached to each question is shown after each question.

You should spend approximately one hour on Section I and 40 minutes on Section II.

You may use a French dictionary.

SECTION I—READING

Read the whole article carefully and then answer **in English** the questions which follow it.

This passage tells us about how young people can get into financial difficulty.

Les Jeunes et leur Argent

C'est avec la rentrée des classes que le déluge de publicité commence. Les étudiants ne seront jamais plus riches qu'à ce moment-là. Après un été de
5 travail payé, ils ont de l'argent à brûler. Argent que des entreprises de toutes sortes lorgnent[1] d'un oeil intéressé.

Les étudiants qui retournent au
10 collège ou à l'université se font bombarder de dépliants et de promesses. Pour le prix d'un téléphone portable, un service Internet ou une carte de crédit, paraît-il, leur
15 popularité et leur bonheur seront garantis. C'est la règle cardinale du marketing jeunesse – offrez-leur un beau petit cadeau super-cool: vidéos exclusives, musique gratuite . . . Et
20 cela vaut la peine: le marché étudiant est d'une grande importance pour les entreprises qui en font de gros profits.

Cette sorte de publicité s'applique partout, mais attire particulièrement
25 les jeunes. Les jeunes d'aujourd'hui contribuent peu aux dépenses familiales, avec le résultat que presque tout leur argent est utilisé pour financer leurs loisirs. Et ils ont
30 tendance à penser que le bonheur, c'est acheter, posséder toujours plus.

Anita, Acheteuse Compulsive

Anita, par exemple, est étudiante de langues vivantes à la fac de Lille. Elle
35 rêve de voyager pour perfectionner ses langues mais elle ne peut rien faire à cause de ses dettes. Pendant les vacances universitaires elle doit toujours trouver un boulot et travailler
40 le plus possible pour avoir un peu d'argent avant la rentrée. Anita explique comment elle a eu ces dettes: «Je ne peux pas résister quand je suis devant une vitrine. Même quand je
45 sais que les articles ne sont pas toujours nécessaires, je dois les acheter tout de suite! Articles de luxe ou produits liés à l'apparence – un sac à main ou de belles chaussures, des
50 parfums ou des bijoux – je les vois, j'en remplis mon panier et je passe à la caisse. Le problème c'est qu'il y a maintenant trop de facilité de paiement quand on paie ses achats
55 avec une carte. Je n'ai qu'à sortir ma carte de crédit pour avoir ce que je veux.» Récemment, Anita a coupé en deux ses cartes et a parlé à un conseiller à la fac qui l'aide à gérer ses
60 affaires.

«Notre société nous encourage à acheter sans penser. Autrefois, le travailleur recevait une enveloppe avec son salaire dedans. Il savait
65 exactement combien il pouvait dépenser. On achetait les choses parce qu'on en avait besoin. Aujourd'hui, l'argent est invisible» dit Anita.

Les principales dettes des étudiants
70

Pour la plupart des étudiants, leurs ennuis financiers commencent avec un contrat de téléphone portable qu'ils ont du mal à respecter. Avant
75 d'entrer dans un contrat de longue durée, il y a quelques précautions utiles à prendre. Voici quelques conseils qu'offre un spécialiste en marketing jeunesse.

«Tout d'abord, renseignez-vous
80 avant d'acheter pour ne pas sauter sur la première offre. Négociez et obtenez le meilleur service et le meilleur prix. Et deuxièmement, rappelez-vous que votre situation financière peut
85 changer, et que l'argent que vous avez

gagné ne durera pas pour toujours. Prenez soin de ne pas avoir de paiements mensuels que vous aurez des difficultés à payer.»

90

Et quelques suggestions pour les parents.

Les parents ont eux aussi des responsabilités. «Techniquement, un

jeune de 17 ans peut signer un contrat de téléphone portable,» affirme un des experts, «mais il ne faut pas hésiter à parler de finances avec son ado. Discutez avec eux des coûts du téléphone portable, et si nécessaire établissez des règles strictes sur son utilisation. C'est comme ça qu'on évitera de gros problèmes plus tard.»

95

100

[1] lorgner = to eye; to look at

QUESTIONS

Marks

1. Businesses try hard to capture the "youth market" in the period after the summer holidays. (lines 1–31)

   (a) Why do businesses choose this particular period to target young people?   **2**

   (b) What promises do the advertising leaflets seem to make?   **2**

   (c) What is the "golden rule" of marketing?   **1**

   (d) Why are young people, in particular, attracted to this sort of advertising?   **3**

2. Anita is an example of a young person who has fallen into debt. (lines 32–68)

   (a) How do her debts prevent Anita from doing what she wants?   **1**

   (b) She explains how she got into so much debt. How did it happen?   **3**

   (c) What problem does Anita see with shopping nowadays?   **1**

   (d) What steps has she taken recently to get out of debt?   **2**

3. Mobile phone contracts are a common cause of young people's debts. (lines 69–103)

   (a) How should young people ensure they get the best deal?   **2**

   (b) What should they try to avoid?   **1**

   (c) What can parents do to help their child avoid making an expensive mistake?   **2**

   (20)

4. Translate into English:

   Notre société . . . dit Anita (lines 61–68)   **10**

   (30)

[Turn over for SECTION II on *Page four*

SECTION II—DIRECTED WRITING

Marks

Last year you were selected to go on a three-month visit to a town in France where you stayed with a French family.

On your return you have been asked to write an account of your experiences **in French** for inclusion in the foreign language section of your school/college magazine.

You must include the following information and **you should try to add** other relevant details:

*   when you went **and** how you got there

*   where the town was situated **and** what it was like

*   how you got on with the French family

*   some of the things you did during your three-month stay

*   what you found to be different about living in France

*   whether you feel it is a good idea to spend three months living with a French family.

Your account should be 150–180 words in length.

Marks will be deducted for any area of information that is omitted.　　　　　**(15)**

[END OF QUESTION PAPER]

X059/303

NATIONAL
QUALIFICATIONS
2010

TUESDAY, 18 MAY
11.00 AM – 12.00 NOON

FRENCH
HIGHER
Listening Transcript

This paper must not be seen by any candidate.

The material overleaf is provided for use in an emergency only (eg the recording or equipment proving faulty) or where permission has been given in advance by SQA for the material to be read to candidates with additional support needs. The material must be read exactly as printed.

Instructions to reader(s):

The dialogue below should be read in approximately 4 minutes. On completion of the first reading, pause for two minutes, then read the dialogue a second time.

Where special arrangements have been agreed in advance to allow the reading of the material, those sections marked **(f)** should be read by a female speaker and those marked **(m)** by a male.

Candidates have two minutes to study the questions before the transcript is read.

Jean is talking to Annie who has just returned from holiday.

(m) **Vous venez de passer les vacances avec vos copines pour la première fois, n'est-ce pas?**

(f) Oui, je suis allée en Espagne avec mes copines. C'était la première fois que nous partions seules sans parents et c'était fantastique! Nous avons fait toutes les réservations nous-mêmes.

(m) **Vous étiez combien dans le groupe?**

(f) On était quatre – quatre filles. Nous nous sommes bien amusées car nous sommes du même âge et dans la même classe et donc nous nous sommes bien entendues ensemble. Nous avons fait des économies pendant un an pour pouvoir partir. Voilà pourquoi on a loué un appartement. C'était moins cher.

(m) **Et vous avez aimé ça, votre appartement?**

(f) Ah oui. Nous n'étions pas obligées de nous lever trop tôt le matin pour le petit déjeuner comme dans un hôtel, et le soir nous pouvions jouer de la musique en bavardant presque toute la nuit. Il y avait même un petit balcon qui donnait sur la piscine et les jardins.

(m) **Il y avait d' autres avantages?**

(f) Oui. On dépense moins pour la nourriture quand on est dans un appartement car on a la possibilité de préparer des plats simples. Ça coûte assez cher de toujours manger au restaurant.

(m) **Et est-ce que vous avez parlé beaucoup espagnol?**

(f) Ah oui, nous avons essayé de perfectionner notre langue. On a fait des efforts pour parler espagnol, d'abord avec la serveuse dans un petit café du coin où on mangeait, et plus tard, le soir, quand on allait en boîte et bavardait avec les garçons qu'on y rencontrait! Mais tout le monde a trouvé notre accent espagnol très amusant.

(m) Vous préférez les vacances comme ça avec vos copines?

(f) Oui, avec les copines on peut choisir ce qu'on veut faire. On peut faire ce qu'on veut quand on veut. Mais, d'un autre côté, quand on part en famille, on a moins de préparatifs à faire, et on se sent plus en sécurité quand les parents sont là.

(m) Donc, vous aimez aussi partir en vacances avec les parents?

(f) Oh, je ne sais pas, parce qu'il y a aussi des inconvénients. C'est surtout à cause de mon père. Il insiste pour qu'on se lève toujours de bonne heure. Et il veut toujours être actif et faire quelque chose. Il s'amuse à faire des photos tout le temps. Il déteste s'asseoir sur la plage.

(m) Alors vous allez partir sans parents à l'avenir?

(f) Au contraire! L'été prochain je ferai un grand voyage en Australie avec mes parents. Ma cousine se marie là-bas et nous a invités. Après le mariage, je voudrais visiter Sydney car on dit que c'est une ville merveilleuse. Je voudrais faire du ski nautique dans la baie, ou peut-être même faire un saut à l'élastique! On ne sait jamais!

Vous voyez – les parents sont toujours utiles quand il s'agit de payer!

[END OF TRANSCRIPT]

[BLANK PAGE]

FOR OFFICIAL USE

Examiner's Marks	
A	
B	

Total
Mark

X059/302

NATIONAL
QUALIFICATIONS
2010

TUESDAY, 18 MAY
11.00 AM – 12.00 NOON

FRENCH
HIGHER
Listening/Writing

Fill in these boxes and read what is printed below.

Full name of centre

Town

Forename(s)

Surname

Date of birth

Day Month Year   Scottish candidate number   Number of seat

Do not open this paper until told to do so.

Answer Section A **in English** and Section B **in French**.

Section A

Listen carefully to the recording with a view to answering, **in English**, the questions printed in this answer book. Write your answers **clearly and legibly** in the spaces provided after each question.

You will have 2 minutes to study the questions before hearing the dialogue for the first time.

The dialogue will be played **twice**, with an interval of 2 minutes between the two playings.

You may make notes at any time but only in this answer book. **Score out any notes before you hand in the book.**

Move on to Section B when you have completed Section A: you will **not** be told when to do this.

Section B

Do not write your response in this book: **use the 4 page lined answer sheet**.

You will be told to insert the answer sheet inside this book before handing in your work.

You may consult a French dictionary at any time during **both** sections.

Before leaving the examination room you must give this book to the Invigilator. If you do not, you may lose all the marks for this paper.

Section A

Marks

Jean is talking to Annie who has just returned from holiday.

1. What was unusual about this holiday for Annie?   1

2. Why had her group got on so well together?   2

3. How had they prepared for the holiday?   1

4. What did they like about their flat?   3

5. How did living in a flat save them money?   1

DO NOT
WRITE IN
THIS
MARGIN

Marks

6. (*a*) What opportunities did they have to practise their Spanish?   **2**

    (*b*) How did people react to their efforts?   **1**

7. (*a*) What did she especially like about holidays with her friends?   **1**

    (*b*) Name **one** advantage of going on holiday with parents that she mentions.   **1**

8. What does she dislike about going on holiday with her dad?   **3**

9. (*a*) What plans does she have for next year's holiday?   **2**

    (*b*) Why is she looking forward to visiting Sydney?   **2**

    (20)

[Turn over for Section B on *Page four*

Marks

Section B

Annie nous parle des vacances.

Quelles sont vos vacances idéales?   Avec ou sans parents?   Actives ou relaxantes?   Donnez vos raisons.

Ecrivez 120-150 mots en français pour exprimer vos idées.

10

(30)

USE THE 4 PAGE LINED ANSWER SHEET FOR YOUR ANSWER TO SECTION B

[END OF QUESTION PAPER]

HIGHER
2011

[BLANK PAGE]

X059/301

NATIONAL QUALIFICATIONS 2011	TUESDAY, 17 MAY 9.00 AM – 10.40 AM	**FRENCH HIGHER** Reading and Directed Writing

45 marks are allocated to this paper. The value attached to each question is shown after each question.

You should spend approximately one hour on Section I and 40 minutes on Section II.

You may use a French dictionary.

SECTION I—READING

Read the whole article carefully and then answer **in English** the questions which follow it.

In this article Hugo Girard, a famous Canadian strongman, talks about his life and his plans to retire from the world of competition.

Hugo Girard prend sa retraite des compétitions d'hommes forts

Après plus de dix ans de compétitions sur la scène internationale, Hugo Girard, un athlète de force, vient d'annoncer sa
5 retraite. Ce géant à la force surhumaine, qui soulève facilement des roches lourdes de cent kilos et qui tire des camions, quitte le monde des hommes forts la tête haute. «Je crois
10 que j'ai gagné le respect des gens du Canada et que je laisse derrière moi l'image d'un homme qui a des valeurs et des principes,» dit-il. «Pour moi, ça, c'est le plus important.»

15 **Il faut faire les bons choix**

Depuis son enfance, Hugo Girard a une passion pour l'entraînement physique. A l'âge de dix ans, il regardait son père s'entraîner dans leur
20 maison. «Pour moi, mon père était l'homme le plus fort du monde, et je rêvais de devenir aussi fort que lui,» raconte Hugo. «Aussi, je lisais beaucoup de bandes dessinées et je
25 m'imaginais être le superhéros.

Mais j'ai fait un bon choix de carrière quand je suis devenu policier dans la ville de Gatineau avant de faire le saut dans le monde des hommes
30 forts. On m'a permis de prendre un congé sans solde et j'ai toujours gardé en tête que j'avais une carrière si je ne réussissais pas dans la compétition.»

La motivation

35 Hugo a repoussé ses limites tout au long de sa vie, et c'est cette motivation de réussir qui a plus impressionné son public. «Je suis comme le boxeur qui tombe au tapis et qui a deux choix:
40 rester à terre ou se relever. Moi, j'ai été blessé plusieurs fois, mais j'ai toujours su trouver le courage

nécessaire pour continuer la compétition et battre des records. La
45 vie est faite d'obstacles, de bons moments et de moins bons moments, mais il faut savoir passer au travers et s'accrocher à ses rêves.»

C'est pour ça que Hugo Girard
50 donne des conférences sur la motivation aux étudiants des écoles secondaires depuis le début de sa carrière d'homme fort. «À travers mon message, je souhaite encourager les
55 jeunes à se surpasser et surtout à croire en eux-mêmes. Je veux leur faire voir qu'on peut réussir de grandes choses tout en étant quelqu'un de bien ordinaire. Il faut seulement faire les
60 bons choix et travailler fort pour réaliser son rêve.»

Les préjugés

Mais même s'il est aujourd'hui l'idole de plusieurs athlètes, Hugo
65 Girard a vécu les préjugés réservés aux sportifs dès son adolescence. «L'image de l'homme sportif typique – beaucoup de talent et pas beaucoup de cerveau – m'a forcé à montrer au
70 public que j'étais autre chose qu'un homme fort. Il y en a plein d'autres qui peuvent soulever une pierre lourde, mais trouver la motivation pour être champion canadien six fois, ça c'est
75 autre chose.»

Changer les perceptions

Maintenant de retour à la vie normale, Hugo sait qu'il y aura la difficulté d'une période d'adaptation, mais il y fera face au moment venu.
80 Pour le moment, il ne pense qu'à passer plus de temps avec ses proches, et surtout avec son fils Tyles qui

entre à la prématernelle cette année.
85 «Mon fils a changé ma perception de la
vie. Aujourd'hui, je sais qu' il y a des
choses plus importantes que d'être
toujours le premier dans tout ce qu'on
fait. A vrai dire, je le savais avant,
90 mais mon fils me l'a fait réaliser
pleinement.»

Et voilà pourquoi Hugo Girard
reprendra son uniforme de policier
dans la Sûreté Municipale de Gatineau
le 15 octobre prochain. «À long terme, 95
j'aimerais travailler dans le secteur des
communications et des relations
publiques de la police. Après tout,
c'est ce que je fais depuis dix ans.»

QUESTIONS
Marks

1. Hugo Girard believes he has had a successful career as a strongman. (lines 1–14)

    (a) What examples are given of Hugo's feats of strength? **2**

    (b) Why does he feel proud of himself? **2**

2. He has been careful when planning out his career. (lines 15–33)

    (a) What were his ambitions when he was a boy? Mention **two** things. **2**

    (b) Why was it a good decision to join the police? Give any **one** reason. **1**

3. Self-motivation is one of his key qualities. (lines 34–61)

    (a) How has Hugo taken inspiration from boxers? **2**

    (b) What is his approach to the difficulties of life? **2**

    (c) What effect does he hope that his seminars will have upon young people? **3**

4. According to Hugo, people often have negative views of sportsmen and women. (lines 62–75)

    (a) What does he think is the view that people have of a typical sportsman? **1**

    (b) How does he think that he has proved himself different from most athletes? **1**

5. He is now about to embark on a new lifestyle. (lines 76–99)

    (a) What are his plans for the immediate future? **1**

    (b) What is he going to do in October? **1**

    (c) What is his long-term ambition, and why? **2**

    (20)

6. Translate into English:

    "Mon fils a changé . . . me l'a fait réaliser pleinement." (lines 85–91) **10**

    (30)

[Turn over for SECTION II on *Page four*

SECTION II—DIRECTED WRITING

Marks

Last summer, you spent 2 months in France, working in a holiday camp for French schoolchildren (une colonie de vacances), where you helped with the activities organised for them. During your stay, you shared accommodation with other student helpers.

On your return from the visit, you have been asked to write an account of your experiences **in French** for inclusion in the foreign language section of your school/college magazine.

You must include the following information and **you should try to add** other relevant details:

- where the camp was **and** how you travelled there
- how you found out about the job
- what you did to help with activities for the children
- what you thought of sharing your accommodation with other students
- what opportunities you had to visit other parts of France
- why you would or would not recommend this type of experience to others.

Your account should be 150–180 words in length.

Marks will be deducted for any area of information that is omitted.

(15)

[END OF QUESTION PAPER]

X059/303

NATIONAL QUALIFICATIONS 2011	TUESDAY, 17 MAY 11.00 AM – 12.00 NOON	**FRENCH** HIGHER Listening Transcript

This paper must not be seen by any candidate.

The material overleaf is provided for use in an emergency only (eg the recording or equipment proving faulty) or where permission has been given in advance by SQA for the material to be read to candidates with additional support needs. The material must be read exactly as printed.

Instructions to reader(s):

The dialogue below should be read in approximately 4 minutes. On completion of the first reading, pause for two minutes, then read the dialogue a second time.

Where special arrangements have been agreed in advance to allow the reading of the material, those sections marked **(f)** should be read by a female speaker and those marked **(m)** by a male.

Candidates have two minutes to study the questions before the transcript is read.

Anaïs is in the final year in her lycée and she is discussing what lies ahead for her.

(m)   **Anaïs, est-ce que ton année de terminale se passe bien?**

(f)   Oui, ça se passe bien. D'abord, en terminale, on étudie seulement les cours qui nous intéressent: par exemple je ne fais plus de sciences parce que j'étudie la littérature. Et en plus, en France on a le droit de quitter l'établissement quand on veut, si on n'a pas classe, sans demander à personne. Notre lycée est à côté d'une forêt, donc on peut aller se promener dans la forêt. Certains élèves préfèrent traîner dans la cour, tandis que d'autres qui n'habitent pas très loin du lycée choisissent de rentrer à la maison.

(m)   **La pensée des examens du bac ne t'inquiète pas?**

(f)   Non, j'étudie la littérature et je suis forte dans cette matière. Je ne voudrais absolument pas rater mon bac parce qu'en ce cas – là, si on n'a pas de bonnes notes au bac, on doit, soit recommencer l'année, soit arrêter les études. Mais je trouverais ça idiot si on arrêtait après six longues années d'études.

(m)   **Et ensuite il faut prendre des décisions pour l'avenir. Y a-t-il quelqu'un qui peut vous aider?**

(f)   Je n'ai pas encore décidé quelle carrière je veux faire, mais il y a des conseillers d'orientation pour nous aider. Heureusement, il y a un conseiller dans tous les lycées, et si on veut lui parler, on peut tout simplement lui demander un rendez-vous. Le conseiller peut mieux nous aider car il nous connaît et il a toutes nos notes.

(m)   **A ton avis, est-ce que les jeunes ont beaucoup de stress maintenant?**

(f)   Oui, mais surtout ceux qui vont à l'université, et en particulier sur le plan financier où on a plus de dettes. Mes amis qui sont déjà à la fac m'ont parlé des difficultés à trouver un appartement à un prix raisonnable et à payer les transports en commun. On a pas mal de difficultés à se débrouiller seul si vos parents n'ont pas les moyens de vous aider. Mais, moi, j'ai de la chance parce que mes parents m'ont dit qu'ils vont me donner 300 euros tous les mois. En plus, quand je rentrerai chez eux en voiture ils me payeront l'essence.

(m)   Est-ce que tu dirais qu'il y a beaucoup de tentations à éviter quand on est étudiant?

(f)   Oui, il y a beaucoup de tentations, surtout pour les étudiants d'université. A mon avis, les plus dangereuses sont la drogue et faire trop la fête. On a toujours des copains qui fument de la drogue et qui font la fête tout le temps, et ce sont deux habitudes qu'il faut éviter à tout prix. Enfin, la drogue, ça peut avoir de mauvaises conséquences pour la santé et si l'on fait la fête tout le temps, on est trop fatigué pour bien travailler.

(m)   Quand tu auras fini tes études à la fac, as-tu l'intention de chercher un emploi immédiatement?

(f)   Bien sûr, à l'avenir je voudrais m'installer quelque part en France et avoir un métier qui me plaît et une maison à la campagne où je pourrais apprécier mon temps libre. Mais avant cela j'ai l'intention de prendre une année sabbatique et de visiter d'autres pays. Bien sûr que tout cela va me coûter encore plus d'argent, et en conséquence, je voudrais rembourser mes dettes le plus tôt possible.

[END OF TRANSCRIPT]

[BLANK PAGE]

FOR OFFICIAL USE

Examiner's Marks	
A	
B	

Total
Mark

X059/302

NATIONAL
QUALIFICATIONS
2011

TUESDAY, 17 MAY
11.00 AM – 12.00 NOON

FRENCH
HIGHER
Listening/Writing

Fill in these boxes and read what is printed below.

Full name of centre

Town

Forename(s)

Surname

Date of birth

Day	Month	Year	Scottish candidate number	Number of seat

Do not open this paper until told to do so.

Answer Section A **in English** and Section B **in French**.

Section A

Listen carefully to the recording with a view to answering, **in English**, the questions printed in this answer book.   Write your answers **clearly and legibly** in the spaces provided after each question.

You will have 2 minutes to study the questions before hearing the dialogue for the first time.

The dialogue will be played **twice**, with an interval of 2 minutes between the two playings.

You may make notes at any time but only in this answer book.   **Score out any notes before you hand in the book.**

Move on to Section B when you have completed Section A: you will **not** be told when to do this.

Section B

Do not write your response in this book: **use the 4 page lined answer sheet.**

You will be told to insert the answer sheet inside this book before handing in your work.

You may consult a French dictionary at any time during **both** sections.

Before leaving the examination room you must give this book to the Invigilator.   If you do not, you may lose all the marks for this paper.

DO NOT
WRITE IN
THIS
MARGIN

Marks

Section A

Anaïs is in the final year in her lycée and she is discussing what lies ahead for her.

1. (*a*) What two things does Anaïs like about being in "terminale"?   **2**

   (*b*) How might students spend their free time during the school day?   **2**

2. (*a*) Why is she not too worried about the "bac" exam?   **1**

   (*b*) What options are there for those students who do not pass?   **2**

3. (*a*) Why is it easy to talk to a careers adviser?   **2**

   (*b*) Why are they in a good position to help you?   **1**

Marks

4. Anaïs talks about young people's money worries.

   (*a*) Mention two ways in which young people spend their money.

   2

   (*b*) How do her own parents plan to help her financially?

   2

5. Anaïs mentions two dangers facing students. What are they and what are their consequences?

   2

6. At the end of her studies, what are her long-term plans?

   2

7. (*a*) What are her immediate plans?

   1

   (*b*) What consequences will this have for her?

   1

   (20)

[Turn over for Section B on *Page four*

DO NOT
WRITE IN
THIS
MARGIN

Marks

Section B

Anaïs nous a parlé de ses expériences au lycée et des problèmes des jeunes. Et vous, est-ce que vous êtes content(e) dans votre lycée/collège? A votre avis, quelles sont les inquiétudes typiques des jeunes personnes d'aujourd'hui?

Ecrivez 120–150 mots en français pour exprimer vos idées.

10

(30)

USE THE 4 PAGE LINED ANSWER SHEET FOR YOUR ANSWER TO SECTION B

[END OF QUESTION PAPER]

[BLANK PAGE]

X059/12/01

NATIONAL QUALIFICATIONS 2012	THURSDAY, 24 MAY 9.00 AM – 10.40 AM	**FRENCH HIGHER** Reading and Directed Writing

45 marks are allocated to this paper. The value attached to each question is shown after each question.

You should spend approximately one hour on Section I and 40 minutes on Section II.

You may use a French dictionary.

SECTION 1 – READING

Read the whole article carefully and then answer **in English** the questions which follow it.

In this passage Florence is talking about her job with the charity organisation 'Petits Princes', which tries to make life happier for children who are ill.

Les Petits Princes

De nos jours un pourcentage important de la population se sent assez stressé par le train-train quotidien. On se lève très tôt pour
5 lutter contre la circulation ou bien on est coincé dans le métro avec des centaines de personnes qui font exactement la même chose. Quand on rentre enfin à la maison familiale
10 vers 20 heures, on trouve le partenaire fatigué aussi après une longue journée de travail pareil. Mais il y a certains gens qui ont réussi à s'échapper de cette situation de plus en plus
15 stressante.

Il y a cinq ans, Florence avait un poste de responsabilité bien payé dans le marketing; maintenant, elle est bénévole à l'association
20 'Petits Princes', qui aide les enfants gravement malades à réaliser leurs rêves.

«J'apporte des moments de bonheur.»

25 Elle raconte son histoire avec passion. «Un jour, j'en ai eu assez de promouvoir des savons. Je voulais donner un autre sens à ma vie.» En quête d'idées sur internet, elle tombe
30 sur le site 'Petits Princes'. «C'était exactement ce que je cherchais,» dit-elle, les yeux brillants, «car je savais que j'allais pouvoir y être utile. Je ne me suis pas trompée!»

35 Et la différence qu'elle fait est facile à voir. Comme tous les bénévoles, elle a à sa charge quarante enfants malades—ses 'petits princes et princesses'—qu'elle suit durant
40 toute leur maladie. Pour fêter leur anniversaire, elle les emmène au spectacle; quand ils se sentent tristes, elle leur apporte sourires et réconfort.

Donc, chaque mois, elle part avec l'un d'eux pour lui offrir un petit moment
45 de bonheur. «Ils ne demandent pas la lune,» nous dit-elle. «Ils sont réalistes et, en règle générale, ont les mêmes passions que tous les enfants!»

Florence se dépense sans compter.
50
«On ne trouvera pas de pessimisme dans notre association,» explique-t-elle. «Certes, il est vrai qu'il y a des bas et des hauts. Souvent on est confronté à la maladie et à la douleur.
55 Mais par contre on sait toujours qu'on donne de l'espoir et du rêve.» Quand on demande à Florence quels sont les plus beaux souhaits qu'elle a réalisés, elle hésite parce qu'il y en a
60 tant. Elle raconte . . . les enfants qui voulaient voir le Père Noël et qu'elle a emmenés à son atelier en Laponie; ce petit garçon passionné de dauphins qui est parti avec elle en Floride;
65 cette petite fille qui a galopé sur les chevaux en Provence avec ses frères et sœurs . . . Florence pourrait parler des heures de tous ces enfants qui ont pu, le temps d'un rêve, oublier
70 leur maladie. Elle reprend la parole: «Réaliser un rêve donne souvent à l'enfant la force de se battre contre la maladie et d'accepter les traitements, parfois très lourds.»
75

Une vie difficile, mais réussie

Aujourd'hui, Florence partage son temps entre l'association et sa famille: «J'ai la chance incroyable d'avoir trouvé un équilibre: pouvoir
80 me consacrer à mes deux filles et faire une activité qui me passionne!» s'enthousiasme-t-elle. Elle se rend deux jours par semaine à l'association pour recevoir les enfants et les
85 familles et se réunir avec les autres

bénévoles. «Heureusement nous avons le soutien d'un psychologue,» précise-t-elle. «C'est indispensable, car il y a parfois des moments difficiles pour les bénévoles. Dans cette association on verse des larmes mais surtout de joie. Et si mes filles me demandent parfois, 'Mais pourquoi n'es–tu pas payée pour ce que tu fais?' je leur réponds alors que mon salaire, c'est le sourire de l'enfant!»

90

95

Questions

Marks

1. Nowadays a large number of people are stressed by the routine of their working day. (lines 1–22)

    (a) How does the author show how stressful the journey to work can be?   2

    (b) When someone returns home from work, what situation might he or she find?   1

    (c) What does the author say about Florence's previous job in marketing?   1

2. Florence speaks about her current job as a volunteer with 'Petits Princes'. (lines 23–43)

    (a) What motivated her to change job?   2

    (b) What did she feel when she saw the job advertised on the 'Petits Princes' website? Mention any **one** thing.   1

    (c) Give **two** examples of how she can make a child's life better.   2

3. Her work with 'Petits Princes' has both low points and high points. (lines 50–75)

    (a) Which low point and which high point does she mention?   2

    (b) What examples does she give of making children's dreams come true?   3

    (c) How can such experiences help an ill child?   2

4. Florence is now contented with her life. (lines 76–97)

    (a) What balance has she achieved in her life?   1

    (b) The organisation employs a psychologist. Why?   1

    (c) What do her daughters sometimes ask her, and how does she answer?   2

    (20)

5. Translate into English:

    « Donc, chaque mois, … les mêmes passions que tous les enfants!» (lines 44–49)   10

    [Turn over for SECTION II on *Page four*   (30)

SECTION II—DIRECTED WRITING

Marks

Last summer, you were one of a group of students who went with your school for two weeks' work experience in France.

On your return from the visit, you have been asked to write an account of your experiences **in French** for inclusion in the foreign language section of your school/college website.

You must include the following information and **you should try to add** other relevant details:

- how many of you went to France **and** where you went

- what job you did **and** how much you earned

- what you had to do in your work experience

- how you got on with the people that you worked with

- what you liked and/or disliked about the job

- if you would now consider working abroad when you are older.

Your account should be 150–180 words in length.

Marks will be deducted for any area of information that is omitted.   **(15)**

[END OF QUESTION PAPER]

X059/12/12

NATIONAL QUALIFICATIONS 2012	THURSDAY, 24 MAY 11.00 AM – 12.00 NOON	**FRENCH** HIGHER Listening Transcript

This paper must not be seen by any candidate.

The material overleaf is provided for use in an emergency only (eg the recording or equipment proving faulty) or where permission has been given in advance by SQA for the material to be read to candidates with additional support needs.   The material must be read exactly as printed.

Instructions to reader(s):

The dialogue below should be read in approximately 4 minutes. On completion of the first reading, pause for two minutes, then read the dialogue a second time.

Where special arrangements have been agreed in advance to allow the reading of the material, those sections marked (f) should be read by a female speaker and those marked (m) by a male.

Candidates have two minutes to study the questions before the transcript is read.

Annie, a student in a French lycée, has just returned to France after spending a term in a Scottish school as part of an exchange. Here she tells us about her experiences.

(m)   **Annie, vous venez de passer trois mois en Ecosse. Est-ce que vous avez profité de votre séjour là-bas?**

(f)   Oui. Le plus grand avantage c'est que j'ai pu améliorer mon anglais. Mais, ce n'est pas surprenant, parce que quand on est tout seul dans un pays et quand on ne connaît personne, on n'a pas d'autre choix que de parler avec les gens, et on apprend la langue en bavardant.

(m)   **Est-ce qu'il y avait d'autres avantages?**

(f)   Un deuxième avantage c'était de voir comment les gens vivent en Ecosse, par exemple ce qu'ils font dans leur temps libre.

(m)   **Est-ce que vous avez trouvé beaucoup de différences entre la vie en Ecosse et la vie en France?**

(f)   Alors, j'ai trouvé que la façon de manger est très différente. En France nous avons deux repas principaux—le déjeuner et le dîner—alors qu'en Ecosse il me semble qu'on mange plus souvent: on grignote presque toute la journée! J'ai donc changé mes propres habitudes: à midi en France je mange toujours à la cantine du lycée; quand j'étais en Ecosse je sortais en ville acheter quelque chose dans un magasin.

(m)   **Qu'est-ce que vous avez pensé de la vie scolaire en Ecosse?**

(f)   Je préfère la journée scolaire en Ecosse parce que je pouvais rentrer à la maison à quinze heures trente tandis qu'en France je ne rentre qu'à dix-sept heures et quelquefois même plus tard. En plus, j'avais moins de devoirs en Ecosse!

(m)   **Pendant ce long séjour, y avait-il des moments difficiles?**

(f)   Oui. Quelquefois je me sentais triste simplement parce que j'avais laissé mes amis en France. C'est normal, n'est-ce pas? Je faisais des efforts pour me faire des amis écossais mais quand on ne parle pas bien la langue, l'accent écossais est parfois difficile à comprendre.

(m)   **Qu'est-ce que vous avez fait pour vous adapter à la vie en Ecosse?**

(f)   Heureusement, j'étais résolue à réussir et j'ai fait un grand effort pour faire beaucoup de connaissances. La famille chez qui je logeais était très sympa et puis au lycée j'ai rencontré beaucoup de gens de mon âge. Le plus important est de se faire des amis. Je me suis inscrite dans toutes sortes de clubs: j'ai participé à des sports d'équipe et j'ai commencé à chanter dans une chorale, ce qui me plaisait beaucoup. Les clubs sont un excellent moyen de connaître les gens.

(m) **Et finalement, êtes-vous contente d'avoir passé ce trimestre en Ecosse?**

(f) Oui, parce que je crois que j'ai beaucoup gagné en confiance en moi, et j'ai appris à me débrouiller seule. Voilà deux choses très importantes pour la vie. Je n'oublierai jamais les gens que j'ai connus là-bas, et les choses que j'ai faites, mais, en fin de compte, il faut avouer que j'étais bien contente de rentrer en France et de revoir mes amis et ma famille!

[END OF TRANSCRIPT]

[BLANK PAGE]

FOR OFFICIAL USE

Examiner's Marks	
A	
B	

Total
Mark

X059/12/02

NATIONAL
QUALIFICATIONS
2012

THURSDAY, 24 MAY
11.00 AM – 12.00 NOON

FRENCH
HIGHER
Listening/Writing

Fill in these boxes and read what is printed below.

Full name of centre

Town

Forename(s)

Surname

Date of birth

Day	Month	Year	Scottish candidate number	Number of seat

Do not open this paper until told to do so.

Answer Section A **in English** and Section B **in French**.

Section A

Listen carefully to the recording with a view to answering, **in English**, the questions printed in this answer book. Write your answers **clearly and legibly** in the spaces provided after each question.

You will have 2 minutes to study the questions before hearing the dialogue for the first time.

The dialogue will be played **twice**, with an interval of 2 minutes between the two playings.

You may make notes at any time but only in this answer book. **Score out any notes before you hand in the book.**

Move on to Section B when you have completed Section A: you will **not** be told when to do this.

Section B

Do not write your response in this book: **use the 4 page lined answer sheet**.

You will be told to insert the answer sheet inside this book before handing in your work.

You may consult a French dictionary at any time during **both** sections.

Before leaving the examination room you must give this book to the Invigilator. If you do not, you may lose all the marks for this paper.

Marks

Section A

Annie, a student in a French lycée, has just returned to France after spending a term in a Scottish school as part of an exchange. Here she tells us about her experiences.

1. (a) What was the biggest advantage for Annie of spending three months in Scotland?   1

   (b) Why was it not surprising that this should happen?   2

2. What second advantage does she mention?   1

3. (a) What differences in eating habits did she find between Scotland and France?   2

   (b) How did her lunchtime eating habits change when she was in Scotland?   2

4. What **two** things did she particularly like about Scottish schools?   2

Marks

5. (*a*) Why did Annie sometimes feel sad?

1

(*b*) What made it difficult for her to make friends at first?

2

6. (*a*) Who helped her to get over this initial difficulty?

2

(*b*) What else did she do to get to know people?

2

7. (*a*) In what **two** ways did she benefit from her stay?

2

(*b*) What is her final comment on her experiences?

1

(20)

[Turn over for Section B on *Page four*

Marks

Section B

Annie nous a expliqué combien ses amis lui ont manqué quand elle était en Ecosse.

Et vous, aimez-vous passer beaucoup de temps avec les copains, ou est-ce que vous préférez être seul(e) de temps en temps? A votre avis, quelles sont les qualités d'un(e) bon(ne) ami(e)?

Ecrivez 120—150 mots en français pour exprimer vos idées.

10

(30)

USE THE 4 PAGE LINED ANSWER SHEET FOR YOUR ANSWER TO SECTION B

[END OF QUESTION PAPER]

[BLANK PAGE]

Acknowledgements

Permission has been sought from all relevant copyright holders and Bright Red Publishing is grateful for the use of the following:

The online version of 'Comment mon blog a change ma vie' by Camille Le Gall taken from www.madamefigaro.fr © Camille Le Gall/Madame Figaro (2008 Reading & Directed Writing pages 2 & 3);

An extract taken from 'Un dur coeur tendre' by Catherine Lamontagne, taken from www.cyberpresse.ca 25 August 2008. Reproduced by permission Le Droit (2011 Reading & Directed Writing pages 2 & 3).

SQA HIGHER FRENCH
2008–2012

SECTION I – Reading

1. (a) Jealousy

or

She saw her friend's/Anuja's

Her friend/Anuja had (started) one (so she wanted one)

(b) • An (elegant) photo on the home-page/opening-/ entry- /welcome-/welcoming- /first-/front- page
   • Of herself (well) made-up/done-up <u>and</u> with a (broad/big/large) smile wearing (a lot of) make-up <u>and</u> smiling

NB: 'She created a very elegant welcome page with her appearing well made-up and with a big smile' = 2 points

2. (a) *Any three from:*
   • Life as a <u>university student of journalism</u>
   • Assessment/review/critique/account of/(critical) essay/ article/report on a Van Gogh <u>exhibition/exposition</u> (at the Metropolitan Museum)
   • (Calling into doubt/questioning) the New York candidature/candidacy/application/ nomination/bid for the 2012 Olympic Games
   New York wanting to host …
   • Her meeting/encounter/time spent/discussion with police/a police patrol/patrol of police/group of police in the streets/a street/in Harlem
   • Photos <u>illustrating each article</u> (that she had taken/from her digital camera)

(b) <u>The French</u> love New York.

or

<u>The French</u> like/are interested in <u>everything to do with</u> NY.

or

She gives/brings them some of the New York atmosphere/ ambiance.

(c) Her descriptions of (her) <u>nights out/parties/ evenings</u> give people a slice/taste/glimpse of/an insight into NY life

(d) Her ego is/she feels flattered/it boosts her ego

or

She thought/thinks herself a superstar of the Internet

3. (a) Give personal/private details/details of private life to strangers/to whoever/to whoever can read them/to anyone you don't know/for the public to see/on the internet/to whoever might stumble upon them/might type random words into a search engine.
   [Give <u>private</u> details to <u>stranger</u>]

(b) • That wasn't enough (for Élodie)/Élodie wanted more details

   or

   Élodie sent numerous/5 e-mails to/ constantly/continuously emailed Camille
   • <u>Camille</u> broke off contact/ceased/stopped replying
   • Élodie('s tone) became less friendly/ warm/hearty/cordial

   or

   She subjected Camille to/sent Camille a <u>flood/torrent/wave/amount</u> of abuse/ insults/threats

4. (a) • He had read her/a review/report of/blog/ comment(s)/remarks/commentary on a film/*Les Choristes*
   • He had/wanted to interview the star <u>and</u> wanted to talk to her

(b) She received a job <u>offer/offer</u> of employment/a (steady) job/work
   The journalist/he <u>offered</u> her a job

(c) *Any three from:*
   • She checks the visitor/viewer statistics/statistics of visits to her blog/how many people have been on/visited/viewed the blog + compulsively/when she wakes/gets up/first thing
   • She hates days when no-one leaves/makes a comment/people don't comment/when she doesn't get comments/remarks
   • She is delighted when a new reader appears/comes forward/joins her blog/is evident/has a look/arises/shows themselves/emerges/turns up/leaves a comment
   • She continually improves/doesn't stop/never stops improving her blog

(d) She thinks that her readers will be inconsolable/ devastated/distraught if/when/that she stops/she goes back to France/she is leaving/her blog ends/without her blog

5. • C' est Andy Warhol qui le disait:
   It is/was Andy Warhol who said (it)/used to say (it)

   • "À l' avenir, chacun aura son quart d' heure de célébrité".
   « *In the future, everyone will have his/their quarter of an hour of fame/celebrity* ».

   • Moi, je suis célèbre depuis plus de quatre mois *(As for me)*
   I have been famous for more than four months.

   • Et qu' ai-je fait pour mériter cette renommée?
   And what have I done to deserve this fame?

   • J' ai tout simplement ouvert mon blog sur Internet.
   I (have) (quite) simply opened my blog on the Internet.

Section II – Directed Writing

All 6 bullet points must be addressed.

2 marks (ie single marks, not pegged ones) will be deducted for each bullet not addressed, up to a maximum of 2 bullets. If 3 or more bullets have not been addressed, the mark will be 0.

After this has been considered, marks are allocated for the essay according to the tables on pages 78-79.

Category	Mark	Content	Accuracy	Language Resource – Variety, Range, Structures
Very Good	15	• All bullet points are covered fully, in a balanced way, including a number of complex sentences. • Some candidates may also provide additional information. • A wide range of verbs/verb forms, tenses and constructions is used. • Overall this comes over as a competent, well thought-out account of the event which reads naturally.	• The candidate handles all aspects of grammar and spelling accurately, although the language may contain some minor errors or even one more serious error. • Where the candidate attempts to use language more appropriate to post-Higher, a slightly higher number of inaccuracies need not detract from the overall very good impression.	• The candidate is comfortable with almost all the grammar used and generally uses a different verb or verb form in each sentence. • There is good use of a variety of tenses, adjectives, adverbs and prepositional phrases and, where appropriate, word order. • The candidate uses co-ordinating conjunctions and subordinate clauses throughout the writing. • The language flows well.
Good	12	• All bullet points are addressed, generally quite fully, and some complex sentences may be included. • The response to one bullet point may be thin, although other bullet points are dealt with in some detail. • The candidate uses a reasonable range of verbs/verb forms and other constructions.	• The candidate generally handles verbs and other parts of speech accurately but simply. • There may be some errors in spelling, adjective endings and, where relevant, case endings. • Use of accents may be less secure. • Where the candidate is attempting to use more complex vocabulary and structures, these may be less successful, although basic structures are used accurately. • There may be minor misuse of dictionary.	• There may be less variety in the verbs used. • Most of the more complex sentences use co-ordinating conjunctions, and there may also be examples of subordinating conjunctions where appropriate. • In one bullet point the language may be more basic than might otherwise be expected at this level. • Overall the writing will be competent, mainly correct, but pedestrian.
Satisfactory	9	• The candidate uses mainly simple, more basic sentences. • The language is perhaps repetitive and uses a limited range of verbs and fixed phrases not appropriate to this level. • In some examples, one or two bullet points may be less fully addressed. • In some cases, the content may be similar to that of good or very good examples, but with some serious accuracy issues.	• The verbs are generally correct, but basic. • Tenses may be inconsistent, with present tenses being used at times instead of past tenses. • There are quite a few errors in other parts of speech – personal pronouns, gender of nouns, adjective endings, cases, singular/plural confusion – and in the use of accents. • Some prepositions may be inaccurate or omitted, eg I went the town. • While the language may be reasonably accurate in three or four bullet points, in the remaining two control of the language structure may deteriorate significantly. • Overall, there is more correct than incorrect and there is the impression overall that the candidate can handle tenses.	• The candidate copes with the past tense of some verbs. • A limited range of verbs is used to address some of the bullet points. • Candidate relies on a limited range of vocabulary and structures. • When using the perfect tense, the past participle is incorrect or the auxiliary verb is omitted on occasion. • Sentences may be basic and mainly brief. • There is minimal use of adjectives, probably mainly after 'is', eg The boss was helpful. • The candidate has a weak knowledge of plurals. • There may be several spelling errors, eg reversal of vowel combinations.

Category	Mark	Content	Accuracy	Language Resource – Variety, Range, Structures
Unsatisfactory	6	• In some cases the content may be basic. • In other cases there may be little difference in content between Satisfactory and Unsatisfactory. • The language is repetitive, with undue reliance on fixed phrases and a limited range of common basic verbs such as *to be, to have, to play, to watch*. • While the language used to address the more predictable bullet points may be accurate, serious errors occur when the candidate attempts to address the less predictable areas. • The Directed Writing may be presented as a single paragraph.	• Ability to form tenses is inconsistent. • In the use of the perfect tense the auxiliary verb is omitted on a number of occasions. • There may be confusion between the singular and plural form of verbs. • There are errors in many other parts of speech – gender of nouns, cases, singular/plural confusion – and in spelling and, where appropriate, word order. • Several errors are serious, perhaps showing mother tongue interference. • There may be one sentence which is not intelligible to a sympathetic native speaker. • One area may be very weak. • Overall, there is more incorrect than correct.	• The candidate copes mainly only with the predictable language required at the earlier bullet points. • The verbs 'was' and 'went' may also be used correctly. • There is inconsistency in the use of various expressions, especially verbs. • Sentences are more basic. • An English word may appear in the writing or a word may be omitted. • There may be an example of serious dictionary misuse.
Poor	3	• The content and language may be very basic. • However, in many cases the content may be little different from that expected at Unsatisfactory or even at Satisfactory.	• Many of the verbs are incorrect or even omitted. • There are many errors in other parts of speech - personal pronouns, gender of nouns, adjective endings, cases, singular/plural confusion - and in spelling and word order. • Prepositions are not used correctly. • The language is probably inaccurate throughout the writing. • Some sentences may not be understood by a sympathetic native speaker.	• The candidate cannot cope with more than one or two basic verbs, frequently 'had' and 'was'. • The candidate displays almost no knowledge of past tenses of verbs. • Verbs used more than once may be written differently on each occasion. • The candidate has a very limited vocabulary. • Several English or 'made-up' words may appear in the writing. • There are examples of serious dictionary misuse.
Very Poor	0	• The content is very basic **or** • The candidate has not completed at least three of the core bullet points.	• (Virtually) nothing is correct. • Most of the errors are serious. • Very little is intelligible to a sympathetic native speaker	• The candidate copes only with 'have' and 'am'. • Very few words are correctly written in the foreign language. • English words are used. • There may be several examples of mother tongue interference. • There may be several examples of serious dictionary misuse.

FRENCH HIGHER
LISTENING/WRITING
2008

SECTION A – Listening

1. (*a*) • As a waitress/server
  or
  She worked/works in a restaurant
  + twice a week/two nights/evenings/days a week
  • As a babysitter/childminder
  or
  She watched/watches/looks after/takes care of
  children/infants
  + on Wednesday(s)/once a week
  (*Each point requires job and when*)

   (*b*) The pay is better (than during the day)/gets more
   money/it's not (as) good pay during the day
   (*Must be idea of comparison*)

2. • To pay for her shopping (trips)/she likes shopping/loves
  shops

   • To learn about/discover/experience/know/get used to the
   world of work/job world/working world/for work
   experience

3. (*a*) • She could <u>play/have fun</u> with the children
   • She could do homework/study <u>while they were asleep/in
   bed/after she put them to bed</u>

   (*b*) • The restaurant job was (very/too/quite) tiring/made her
   tired
   • You had to <u>smile all the time/always</u>

4. (*a*) They were out for a good time/having fun/to relax
  or
  They were with their family <u>and/or</u> friends
  (*need verb or both groups of people*)

   (*b*) They left <u>good/a lot of/more</u> tips

5. • They were the same/similar age(s)

   • They were working/were there for the same/similar reasons

6. • It was difficult to <u>motivate herself/be/stay motivated</u> after a
  (long) day <u>studying/at school</u>

   • <u>Child-minding/baby-sitting/working with children/looking
   after children</u> brings a lot of responsibilities/demands a lot
   of care/attention. She had a lot of responsibility looking
   after children.
   You need to be responsible looking after children.
   She has to take responsibility for the children.
   (*childminding linked to responsibility/care/attention*)

7. (*a*) They thought her studies/school work might suffer/she
  won't have time to study/her studies should come first.
  School work/grades is/are/was/were suffering Parents are
  worried about her schoolwork/ grades/worried she is not
  studying.
  (*Key idea: general schoolwork/performance*)

   (*b*) • She did <u>extra/additional/supplementary
   studying/work/school work/lessons</u> at the weekends
   • She stopped working/gave up her job/did not work (in
   the restaurant) when her exams were getting
   near/approaching/in the run-up to her exams/before her
   exams/when exams were close.
   She stopped working until exams were over.
   She worked until exams were close

8. • Brought her happiness/made her happy
  or
  <u>She realised</u> there are more important things than making
  money

   • She (still) sees the children (every day/always)
   or
   Children (will/do) remember her/think of her

SECTION B – Writing

Task
Short essay
Assessment Process
With reference to *Content, Accuracy and Language Resource*, the
overall quality of the response will be assessed and allocated a
pegged mark.
(See tables on pages 81-82 for details)

Category	Mark	Content	Accuracy	Language Resource – Variety, Range, Structures
Very Good	10	• The topic is covered fully, in a balanced way, including a number of complex sentences. • Some candidates may also provide additional information. • A wide range of verbs/verb forms and constructions is used. There may also be a variety of tenses. • Overall this comes over as a competent, well thought-out response to the task which reads naturally.	• The candidate handles all aspects of grammar and spelling accurately, although the language may contain some minor errors or even one more serious error. • Where the candidate attempts to use language more appropriate to post-Higher, a slightly higher number of inaccuracies need not detract from the overall very good impression.	• The candidate is comfortable with almost all the grammar used and generally uses a different verb or verb form in each sentence. • There is good use of a variety of tenses, adjectives, adverbs and prepositional phrases and, where appropriate, word order. • The candidate uses co-ordinating conjunctions and subordinate clauses throughout the writing. • The language flows well.
Good	8	• The topic is addressed, generally quite fully, and some complex sentences may be included. • The candidate uses a reasonable range of verbs/verb forms and other constructions.	• The candidate generally handles verbs and other parts of speech accurately but simply. • There may be some errors in spelling, adjective endings and, where relevant, case endings. • Use of accents may be less secure. • Where the candidate is attempting to use more complex vocabulary and structures, these may be less successful, although basic structures are used accurately. • There may be minor misuse of dictionary.	• There may be less variety in the verbs used. • Most of the more complex sentences use co-ordinating conjunctions, and there may also be examples of subordinating conjunctions where appropriate. • At times the language may be more basic than might otherwise be expected at this level. • Overall the writing will be competent, mainly correct, but pedestrian.
Satisfactory	6	• The candidate uses mainly simple, more basic sentences. • The language is perhaps repetitive and uses a limited range of verbs and fixed phrases not appropriate to this level. • The topic may not be fully addressed. • In some cases, the content may be similar to that of good or very good examples, but with some serious accuracy issues.	• The verbs are generally correct, but basic. • Tenses may be inconsistent. • There are quite a few errors in other parts of speech – personal pronouns, gender of nouns, adjective endings, cases, singular/plural confusion – and in the use of accents. • Some prepositions may be inaccurate or omitted, eg I go the town. • While the language may be reasonably accurate at times, the language structure may deteriorate significantly in places. • Overall, there is more correct than incorrect and there is the impression overall that the candidate can handle tenses.	• The candidate copes with the present tense of most verbs. • A limited range of verbs is used. • Candidate relies on a limited range of vocabulary and structures. • Where the candidate attempts constructions with modal verbs, these are not always successful. • Sentences may be basic and mainly brief. • There is minimal use of adjectives, probably mainly after 'is', eg My friend is reliable. • The candidate has a weak knowledge of plurals. • There may be several spelling errors, eg reversal of vowel combinations.

Category	Mark	Content	Accuracy	Language Resource – Variety, Range, Structures
Unsatisfactory	4	• In some cases the content may be basic. • In other cases there may be little difference in content between Satisfactory and Unsatisfactory. • The language is repetitive, with undue reliance on fixed phrases and a limited range of common basic verbs such as *to be, to have, to play, to watch*. • While the language used to address the more predictable aspects of the task may be accurate, serious errors occur when the candidate attempts to address a less predictable aspect. • The Personal Response may be presented as a single paragraph.	• Ability to form tenses is inconsistent. • In the use of the perfect tense the auxiliary verb is omitted on a number of occasions. • There may be confusion between the singular and plural form of verbs. • There are errors in many other parts of speech – gender of nouns, cases, singular/plural confusion – and in spelling and, where appropriate, word order. • Several errors are serious, perhaps showing mother tongue interference. • There may be one sentence which is not intelligible to a sympathetic native speaker. • Overall, there is more incorrect than correct.	• The candidate copes mainly only with predictable language. • There is inconsistency in the use of various expressions, especially verbs. • Sentences are more basic. • An English word may appear in the writing or a word may be omitted. • There may be an example of serious dictionary misuse.
Poor	2	• The content and language may be very basic. • However, in many cases the content may be little different from that expected at Unsatisfactory or even at Satisfactory.	• Many of the verbs are incorrect or even omitted. • There are many errors in other parts of speech – personal pronouns, gender of nouns, adjective endings, cases, singular/plural confusion – and in spelling and word order. • Prepositions are not used correctly. • The language is probably inaccurate throughout the writing. • Some sentences may not be understood by a sympathetic native speaker.	• The candidate cannot cope with more than 1 or 2 basic verbs, frequently 'has' and 'is'. • Verbs used more than once may be written differently on each occasion. • The candidate has a very limited vocabulary. • Several English or 'made-up' words may appear in the writing. • There are examples of serious dictionary misuse.
Very Poor	0	• The content is very basic.	• (Virtually) nothing is correct. • Most of the errors are serious. • Very little is intelligible to a sympathetic native speaker.	• The candidate copes only with 'have' and 'am'. • Very few words are correctly written in the foreign language. • English words are used. • There may be several examples of mother tongue interference. • There may be several examples of serious dictionary misuse.

FRENCH HIGHER READING AND DIRECTED WRITING 2009

SECTION I–Reading

1. (a) • the smart/chic/stylish/fashionable/nice/posh/well-off residences/houses/homes/blocks of flats/housing estates
    or
    smart/chic/stylish/fashionable/nice/posh/well-off residents/people living in suburbs
    • people (of the woods) live in camps/a camp/camp-sites/encampments
    or
    people (of the woods) live with difficulty/in difficulty/struggle to survive/have a difficult life

   (b) • they live some distance/far away/distant from one another
    or
    each group has/keeps its own territory/patch

   (c) • It can resist/withstand/tolerate/stand up to strong/80kph wind(s)
    or
    it is solid/strong/sturdy/stable enough to resist the wind(s)

   (d) • the beds are made and the blankets/covers/sheets tidied/put away/well-arranged/nicely folded/well laid-out/in a neat row/orderly
    or
    The beds and covers are tidy

   (e) • the shack is built out of what other people have thrown away
    or
    home is made using recycled materials/from society's waste/from the waste of the inhabitants of the town
    • they have (recovered) a (nice/broken) table from the (village) dump/waste-site/waste depot/scrap yard/scrap warehouse
    or
    table that had been salvaged/thrown away/ discarded

2. (a) • they live/lead (very) isolated lives/a life of isolation/they are isolated
    they are reluctant to accept help
    or
    • they don't accept help willingly/readily/easily

   (b) • Offers/gives them breakfast **or** use of the washing machine/allows to wash clothes (once a week)
    • Offers/gives them (a) Christmas parcel(s)/present(s)

   (c) • none is being built/not building anymore/haven't built any more
    • what there is/was, is being/has been demolished/knocked down/torn down

   (d) • (small) businesses/employers/enterprises/don't want/distrust them/are wary/suspicious of them because they have no fixed address/no house/no permanent home/are homeless
    or
    Employers want people who have fixed accommodation

   (e) • a day here and a day there/occasional days/the occasional day/ casual work
    or
    a job here and there/odd jobs/the odd job on (building/construction) sites/as seasonal workers

3. (a) • the spring/source/stream/water they use gets cold in winter
    or
    They get/it gets cold in winter because they wash by hand/use the spring/source/stream

   (b) • (their) candles can set fire to their cabin/shack

   (c) • their fire can be put out/ruined by the rain
    or
    there is a problem with their fire when it rains/the fire goes out when it rains

4. • despite difficulties/despite everything/despite difficult life it has/allows/permits moments of friendship/friendliness/friendly moments

5. A proximité, on aperçoit la niche de leurs chiens,

   Nearby, you can spot/glimpse the kennel for their dogs,

   deux beaux animaux qui montent la garde.

   two fine/beautiful animals that keep watch/stand guard.

   Un peu plus loin ils ont leur petit jardin potager:

   A little further on they have their little vegetable garden:

   pas facile à faire pousser les légumes en pleine forêt,

   (it is) not easy to grow vegetables in the middle of the forest,

   mais ils y arrivent.

   but they manage/get there.

SECTION II – Directed Writing

Please see the notes for Higher French 2008 Directed Writing on pages 77-79

SECTION A – Listening

1. Last year
   - she enjoyed/liked her first year/had a wonderful/great/happy/good time/year
   or
   she was in the country(side)/at a country school/college
   This year
   - she wants/wanted to have a different experience/to experience a different way of life
   or
   she wanted to live/she is in the town/city

2. (a) **Friends in Scotland**
   - Making/finding/having friends
   or
   New friends/newly-found friends/Scottish friends/friends in Scotland

   (b) **Decision about career**
   - Has helped her decide/choose/know/has confirmed what she wants to do in the future/in her career/in life
   or
   Has persuaded her/She wants to be a teacher

3. - It is hard/difficult/demanding
   or
   It is harder than you think
   It needs/requires/demands/the children need (lots of) patience/understanding
   or
   You have to be patient/understanding

4. (a) - To share/pass on/impart her passion/love for languages/language/her subject/English/French/to make them excited about languages

   (b) - To organise a class/classes/a classroom/deal with problems of organisation/to have organising/ organisational skills
   - To avoid/prevent/stop discipline problems/bad behaviour/indiscipline

5. - It is/She wanted to live in an English-speaking country/town; they speak English there
   - To see/go to/visit the (Scottish) scenery/landscape/ mountains
   or
   Noun + adjective
   The scenery/landscape/countryside/mountains is/are spectacular/outstanding/magnificent
   - (She was interested in) Scottish history/its history/the history of Scotland

6. (a) *Any one from:*
   - She has/had a/catches a cold/colds/It gives her a cold
   or
   - She gets depressed/It is depressing/It depresses her/makes her feel down/gloomy/miserable

   (b) - (She knows) it is bad for her health but she likes it/eats it anyway/it is unhealthy but nice

   (c) - they drop/throw away litter/lots of paper/things on the ground/they litter/do not use bins/they leave rubbish on the ground

7. (a) - her parents phone her every week
   - she contacts/speaks with her friends by MSN/instant messages/goes on MSN with friends/uses MSN to chat with friends/she MSNs her friends

   (b) - (In France) the cat is (always) happy to see her (when she comes back at night)/cat greets/welcomes/comes to see her

8. - they close/are open/late/later/longer/at 8pm/you can shop later
   - there is a better/bigger/larger/more choice/range/variety of (elegant) clothes

SECTION B – Writing

Please see the notes for Higher French 2008 Writing on pages 80–82.

FRENCH HIGHER READING AND DIRECTED WRITING 2010

SECTION I–Reading

1. (a) • Because they have been <u>working</u> (all summer)
   • they will never be richer/better off/wealthier/they are rich/wealthy
   or
   they have money/cash to burn/blow/spend/use up/they have lots of/more/extra money
   (idea of "extra"/"disposable" money)

   (b) • <u>For the price of/if they have/with</u> a mobile/an internet service/a credit card
   (idea of "if they buy …")
   • Popularity <u>and</u> happiness/pleasure (will be/is guaranteed/assured)
   or
   You will become/it will make you popular <u>and</u> happy

   (c) • <u>Give/Offer</u> them a gift(s)/present(s)/video(s)/ music

   (d) • They contribute <u>little/a little/a bit/less</u> to the <u>family</u> expenses/spending/expenditure
   • they can use their money for leisure/hobbies/free time/spare time/activities
   • They think that happiness comes from buying/possessing/owning (more things)

2. (a) • She cannot/wants to travel/have holiday <u>to</u> improve/perfect/study languages
   or
   She has to work <u>during the holidays</u>

   (b) • She cannot resist/is tempted to/has to buy what she sees in/when she passes/is in front of <u>shop/shop window</u>
   • She buys things she doesn't need/unnecessary things/articles/items
   • She buys/fills her basket with luxury items or/and products linked to/which enhance her appearance/ beauty products (both required)
   or all four items of:
   handbag(s); shoes; perfume; jewellery
   or
   luxury items + 2 examples of the four

   (c) • (Too/So) <u>easy</u> to pay by/with credit <u>card</u>/She just has to take out her credit card/paying by credit card makes it easy

   (d) • She has cut her card(s) up/in two/in half
   • She has spoken to a counsellor/advisor/consultant
   or
   She got financial advice

3. (a) • They should do some research/make enquiries/ask for/get information (before buying)
   or
   Not jump at/settle for/leap at/accept/take the first offer
   • Negotiate/Haggle to get the best/a better service <u>and</u> the best/a better price

   (b) • (taking on) monthly payments they cannot afford/pay/have difficulty with/that get you into difficulty/because financial situation could change
   or
   Not jump at/settle for/leap at/accept/take the first offer (provided not given as answer to 3(a))

   (c) • Discuss the costs/expenses/rates of the phone
   or
   Talk to them about finances
   • Set up/establish rules on how the phone is used/on usage/on utilisation

Translation into English

4. UNIT 1

"Notre société nous encourage à acheter sans penser.	"Our society encourages us to buy without thinking.
"Notre société	"Our society
nous encourage	encourages/is encouraging us
à acheter	to buy
sans penser.	without thinking/thought.

UNIT 2

Autrefois, le travailleur recevait une enveloppe avec son salaire dedans.	In the past, the worker received an envelope with his salary inside.
Autrefois,	In the past/the old(en) days/days gone by/other times/Years ago/ Formerly/Once/Before,
le travailleur	the/a worker/working man/ person/employee
recevait une enveloppe	received/got would/used to/receive/get would have received an/one envelope/pay packet
avec son salaire dedans.	with his/his or her salary/wages/pay inside/in it. containing his salary.

UNIT 3

Il savait exactement combien il pouvait dépenser.	He knew exactly how much he could spend.
Il savait	He knew/would/used to know
exactement combien	exactly how much/the exact amount (that)
il pouvait dépenser.	he could/was able to/would be able to/had to spend.

UNIT 4

On achetait les choses parce qu'on en avait besoin.	One/You bought things because one/you needed them.
On achetait les choses	One/You/They/People/ We bought/used to/would buy things
parce qu'	because
on en avait besoin.	one/you/they/people/we needed/would need/had need of/needed to have <u>them</u>.

UNIT 5

Aujourd'hui, l'argent est invisible," dit Anita.	Today, money is invisible," says Anita.
Aujourd'hui,	Today/Nowadays/These days
l'argent est invisible,"	money/the money is invisible/unseen,"
dit Anita.	says Anita.

SECTION II – Directed Writing

Please see the notes for Higher French 2008 Directed Writing on pages 77-79

FRENCH HIGHER LISTENING/WRITING 2010

SECTION A – Listening

1. • It was the <u>first</u> (time/holiday/year) without her parents/family/alone/with her friends/alone with her friends
   or
   they had made all the reservations themselves

2. • They were of the same age
   • They were (all) in the same class(es)/in her class(es)

3. • They had saved up (for a year/all year)

4. • They did not (have to) get up/wake up (early) for breakfast **or** as in a hotel
   • They could play/listen to music/chat/gossip/talk/ speak (almost) all night/late at night/into the night/till late/late in the evening
   They could stay up late chatting
   • There was a balcony **and** (a) pool/garden(s)
   • They could cook meals

5. • They spent less/saved money on food
   or
   they could cook/prepare (simple) meals or food/eat in/it was self-catering
   or
   they did not have to go to restaurants/eat out/ restaurants are expensive

6. (a) • When ordering (food)/With the waitress(es)/ waiter(s)/server(s)/staff in the/a <u>local/nearby</u> café(s)/on the corner **or** <u>that they ate in</u>
   • With a/the boy(s)/(young) man/men (whom they met) at the (night) club/disco

   (b) • They found the girls' (Spanish) <u>accent/ pronunciation</u> amusing/funny/entertaining

7. (a) • You can do <u>what</u> you want/choose <u>what</u> to do, <u>when</u> you want to

   (b) • You feel/It is safe/safer/secure/more secure/It gives security (when they are there)
   or
   There are fewer preparations to make/do/You have to prepare less/they do the preparations

8. *Any three from:*
   • He insists that they get/she gets up early
   or
   They have/She has to get up early

   • He wants to be busy/active/doing something all the time/always
   or
   He wants to do lots of things/activities/He hates doing nothing

   • He takes photos <u>all the time</u>/He is <u>always</u> taking photos
   or
   He takes loads/lots of photos
   or
   He takes photos of everyone/everything

   • He hates/detests (sitting on/going to) the beach

9. (a) • (A long/big/grand trip) with her parents to Australia
   • (invited) to her cousin's wedding

   (b) • (she is told) it is (a) marvellous/wonderful/great/ amazing (city)
   • To water-ski (in the bay)/do a bungee jump

SECTION B – Writing

Please see the notes for Higher French 2008 Writing on pages 80-82.

FRENCH HIGHER READING
AND DIRECTED WRITING
2011

SECTION I – Reading

1. (a) • (Easily) lifts/lifted/picks/picked up rock(s)/heavy
       stone(s)/boulder(s) weighing a hundred kilos
       or
       100 kilos of rocks/stones
       • Pulls/pulled/drags/dragged (some) lorries/a lorry/truck(s)

   (b) • He has/He has won/He gets (lots of/the) respect of (the
       people of/in) Canada/Canadians
       • He is seen as/He has left/leaves the image of a man
       with/having standards/values/principles

2. (a) • To be/become/becoming/being as strong as/like his
       father/dad/a strongman like his dad
       • Being (like) a/the superhero(es) in his comic books/
       cartoons
       or
       He read comics/cartoons and wanted to be like a/the
       superhero(es)

   (b) • They allowed him to take unpaid leave/time off/days off
       without pay (**not**: a holiday without pay)
       or
       • (He knew) he (always/still) had a(nother) career if he was
       not successful (in competitions)/He had a career to return
       to/to fall back on/could come back to the job

3. (a) • When they are knocked down/fall, they can stay down/on
       the ground/on the carpet or get up/By choosing to get
       back up when he is knocked down
       • Despite being injured/hurt/wounded (several times) he
       (always) gets back up, he has (always) (found the courage
       to) come back/continue

   (b) • (You have to know how to) get/pass/work through/
       beyond obstacles/difficulties/good and bad times
       • Hold/hang/cling onto/follow/persevere with/reach for
       your dream(s)

   (c) • Encourage young people to excel/believe in/surpass/outdo
       themselves
       • (Let them see that) you can succeed/achieve (big things)
       while still being an ordinary person/someone who is
       ordinary
       • Help them/(make them see that) you (only) need to make
       the right/good choices/decisions and work
       hard/well/strong

4. (a) • (Lots of) talent **and** not a lot of brains/not very
       smart/clever/not much of a brain/intelligence/no brains

   (b) • (Others can lift heavy weights, but) he has been
       determined/motivated enough to be/has become 6 time
       champion (of Canada)

5. (a) • Spend (lots of/more) time with his family/relatives/close
       ones/next of kin/his son/Tyles

   (b) • Re-join/return to the police/going back to work for the
       police/pick up/go back/return to his police uniform

   (c) • To work in the communications and public relations
       branch
       • Because he has been doing this/something similar for 10
       years

Translation into English

6. UNIT 1

«Mon fils a changé ma perception de la vie.	My son has changed my view of life.
Mon fils	My son/boy
a changé	(has) changed
ma perception de la vie.	my view/perception of/on life my outlook/perspective on life

UNIT 2

Aujourd'hui, je sais qu'il y a des choses plus importantes que	Today, I know that there are more important things than
Aujourd'hui,	Today/Nowadays/These days
je sais qu'	I know (that)
il y a	there are
des choses plus importantes que	more important things (in life) than (some) things (which are) more important than

UNIT 3

d'être toujours le premier dans tout ce qu'on fait	always to be/being first in everything you do
d'être toujours	always to be/come/being/coming
le premier	(the) first/top/number one/best/in first place
dans tout ce qu'on fait	in everything/all (that)/whatever you/we do/one does

UNIT 4

A vrai dire, je le savais avant,	To tell the truth, I knew it before,
A vrai dire,	Truth be told/It's true to say/To tell (you) the truth/(I can) truly/truthfully (say)/Truth to tell/To be honest
je le savais avant,	I knew/did know ((about)it/that/this)before/already

UNIT 5

Mais mon fils me l'a fait réaliser pleinement»	But my son made me realise it fully".
Mais mon fils	But/However my son/my boy
me l'a fait réaliser	(has) made me realise it/that/this
pleinement»	fully/completely/clearly

SECTION II – Directed Writing

Please see the notes for Higher French 2008 Directed Writing on pages 77-79

Please see the notes for Higher French 2008 Directed Writing on pages 77-79

FRENCH HIGHER LISTENING/WRITING 2011

SECTION A – Listening

1. (a) • Students (only) take/choose/she takes/chooses the class(es)/subject(s) they are/she is **interested** in/that they like/want (to do).
   She can drop subject(s) she doesn't like.
   She doesn't study science because she has chosen literature
   (Takes/chooses/studies) **interesting** subject(s)
   • Students can leave (the school) (building)/go home <u>if they have no classes/without asking (for permission)</u>.

   (b) *Any two from:*
   • Walk in the forest/Going for (a) walk(s)
   • <u>Hang around/out/dawdle/walk about/stay</u> in the <u>playground/yard/open area/school grounds/ campus</u>
   • <u>Return/Go</u> home (if they live near school/and study)

2. (a) • She's studying literature and she's good at that/it's her strongest/best subject(s)
   She is strong in/good at literature/her subject(s)
   She (always) gets good marks in literature/her subject(s)

   (b) • Repeat/Re-do/Re-start the year/bac/Try again/Re-sit exam next year/Take exam (again) <u>next year</u>
   • Abandon/Stop/Quit/Leave/End/Give up their studies/course/studying (altogether).
   Leave school/education

3. (a) • There are advisers in <u>every</u> school/college/They are in <u>all</u> schools/colleges/<u>Every</u> school/college has advisers
   • You just have/It is easy to make/to ask for/ request/arrange/get an appointment/a meeting/a time to meet up
   Careers advisers are available to make an appointment/ meeting

   (b) • They know you/all about you
   or
   They know/have your marks/grades

4. (a) • (Renting/Paying/Buying/Finding) lodging/ accommodation/an apartment/flat/a place to stay (at a reasonable price)
   • (Public) transport

   (b) • Give her <u>300</u> (euros) <u>a/every month</u>
   • Fill her car with/Pay for <u>petrol/fuel</u> (when she comes home)

5. • <u>Drugs</u> can have bad consequences for your <u>health</u>
   <u>Drugs</u> cause <u>bad health</u>

   • <u>Partying</u> (too much)/<u>Parties/Celebrations/Clubbing</u> can make you too <u>tired</u>/affect your <u>work/study</u>

   Drugs and partying <u>can affect your health and make you tired</u> – **2 marks**
   Drugs taken at parties <u>can affect your health and make you tired</u>– **1 mark**

6. *Any two from:*
   • To <u>settle</u> (down)/<u>move to</u> somewhere <u>in France</u>
   • Find a job that she <u>likes to do/enjoys/in the area/field she wants</u>
   • Settle down/Move to/Have a house/Live/<u>in the country/ countryside</u>

- Enjoy/Appreciate her <u>free time/leisure time</u>

7. (a) • Take a gap/sabbatical year/year out/see/visit other/lots of/different/foreign countries

 (b) • **Money** It will cost (her) more money/a lot of/lots of money/It will be expensive (for her)
 or
  • **Debt** She will be in debt/will have debts to pay back/refund/meet.
   She will have debt to pay back

SECTION B – Writing

Please see the notes for Higher French 2008 Writing on pages 80-82.

Please see the notes for Higher French 2008 Writing on pages 80-82.

FRENCH HIGHER READING AND DIRECTED WRITING 2012

SECTION I – Reading

1. (a) • Getting/being/waking up/leaving <u>early</u> to fight/struggle against/avoid/beat the <u>traffic</u>
  • being crushed/jammed/squashed in the metro/train
 or
  being/stuck with <u>hundreds/lots of/about</u> a hundred people (doing the same thing) in the metro/train

 (b) • <u>Partner/spouse</u> is tired after a similar day/a long day('s work)

 (c) • it was responsible <u>and</u> well paid

2. (a) • (one day) she had had enough/was fed up of <u>promoting soap(s)</u>
  • she wanted to give her life another/different/new/more meaning/direction/sense/purpose/she wanted to do something meaningful with her life

 (b) • It was exactly/just what/the exact job she was looking for
 or
  she knew that <u>she</u> could be useful/helpful

 (c) • on their <u>birthday</u>, she can take them/they go to <u>(a) show(s)/the theatre</u>
  • when they are (feeling) <u>sad/gloomy/unhappy</u>, <u>she</u> can bring them smiles/<u>she</u> can make them smile/<u>she</u> can comfort/reassure them

3. (a) • you are/she is (often) confronted by/faced with/you/she witness(es)/see(s) illness/sickness/disease <u>and</u> pain/grief/distress
 or
  the children are (often) ill/sick <u>and</u> in pain/grief/distress
  • you are/she/it is giving/providing(the children) hope(s) <u>and</u> (a) dream(s)

 (b) • she took/takes/taking children (who wanted)/children went to see Santa to/in his workshop/to Lapland
  • (a) (little) boy(s), who was crazy/passionate/mad about dolphins, went with her to Florida
 or
  (she took) (a) (little) boy(s) to Florida to see/because of the dolphins
  • (she took) (a) (little) girl(s) horse-riding/galloping in Provence <u>with her brother(s) and sister(s)</u>

 (c) • give(s) them the strength/force/power to fight/combat/tackle their illness
 or
  they forget (about) their illness
  • (help(s) them/give(s) them the strength to) accept their (heavy) treatment(s)

4. (a) • she can devote/dedicate herself/her time to her (two) girls/daughters/children/family <u>and</u> do a job/occupation/work/something/(an) activity(-ies) <u>she loves/is passionate about/fascinates her</u>

 (b) • there can be difficult moments/it provides support <u>for the volunteers/(voluntary) workers</u>

 (c) • why are you/is she not paid?
  • my/her salary/payment is the child's/children's smile(s)

Translation into English

6. UNIT 1

Donc, chaque mois, elle part avec l'un d'eux	Therefore, each month, she leaves with one of them
Donc,	Therefore/So
chaque mois,	each/every month
elle part	she leaves/goes (away/off)
avec l'un d'eux	with one of them she takes one of them away with her

UNIT 2

pour lui offrir un petit moment de bonheur.	to offer/give him/her/ them a little moment of happiness.
pour lui offrir	to offer/give him/her/ them
un petit moment	a/one (little/small) moment
de bonheur.	of happiness/joy/pleasure to treat them to a little moment of happiness

UNIT 3

« Ils ne demandent pas la lune, » nous dit-elle.	"They don't ask (for) the moon/earth," she tells us.
« Ils ne demandent pas	"They don't ask/aren't asking (for)/cry(ing) for
la lune, »	the moon/earth/world,"
nous dit-elle.	she tells us/says to us.

UNIT 4

« Ils sont réalistes et, en règle générale,	"They are realists/ realistic and, as a general rule,
« Ils sont réalistes	"They are realistic/ realists
et, en règle générale,	and, as a (general) rule,

UNIT 5

ont les mêmes passions que tous les enfants ! »	(they) have the same passions as all children."
ont les mêmes passions	have /share the same passions/enthusiasms
que tous les enfants ! »	as all (of/the) children/ kids/youngsters/every child!" [addition of "have"/"do"]

SECTION II – Directed Writing

Please see the notes for Higher French 2008 Directed Writing on pages 77-79

FRENCH HIGHER LISTENING/WRITING 2012

SECTION A – Listening

1. (a) • she (was able to) improve(d)/perfect(ed)/ make/made progress with/was better at her English/her English improved

   (b) • when you are on your own/alone/do not know anyone she was on her own/she didn't know anyone
   • you have to/she had to talk/speak (English) to people [NB "young people" does not negate the point]
   or
   you learn/she learnt by chatting/talking

2. • seeing/experiencing how Scots people live/(the way of) life in Scotland
   or
   what (Scottish) people do in their spare time.

3. (a) • French have 2 main meals/lunch/dinner and dinner/tea
   • Scots eat more often/nibble/snack (almost) all day/all the time

   (b) • in France she eats/ate in the school/canteen/*cantine*/ cafeteria
   • in Scotland she went into town/to a/the shop(s)/down/up the street/she buys/bought something in a/the shop(s)

4. • she could go/got home/leave/left school at 3.30/15.30
   +
   instead of 5.00/17.00
   or
   which is earlier (than in France)
   • less/not (as) much/not a lot of homework

5. (a) • She had left (all) her friends (behind/in France)/she missed/didn't have her friends

   (b) • when you don't/as she did not speak the language/English (very) well/her English wasn't (very) good/fluent/she didn't know a lot of English
   • the (Scottish) accent is (sometimes)/can be difficult to understand

6. (a) • the host/exchange family/family/people she lived with
   • (the) people of her age at school/her classmates

   (b) • *Any two from:*
   joined/was in/took part in/went to all sorts/kinds/types of/a variety of/(lots of) different clubs
   • played team sports/joined sports teams
   • joined/sang in a/the choir/chorus

7. (a) • she gained in (self-)confidence (in herself)/became more confident
   • she learned to get by/survive/cope/manage on her own/independently/to rely on/look after herself/do things by herself

   (b) • she was/is glad/happy/pleased/content/it was/is good to get back to her family and her friends/to see her family and friends (again)

SECTION B – Writing

Please see the notes for Higher French 2008 Writing on pages 80-82.